Audrey Hepburn

First published in the United States in 2007 by Chronicle Books LLC.
First published in Great Britain in 2006 by Boxtree, an imprint of Pan Macmillan Publishers Ltd.

Page 166 constitutes a continuation of the copyright page.

Library of Congress Cataloging-in-Publication Data available.
ISBN-10: 0-8118-5802-2
ISBN-13: 978-0-8118-5802-1

Manufactured in Great Britain

Art direction and design by Graham Marsh
Cover design by Brett MacFadden and Graham Marsh
Front cover artwork by Robert E. McGinnis

Distributed in Canada by Raincoast Books
9050 Shaughnessy Street
Vancouver, British Columbia V6P 6E5

10 9 8 7 6 5 4 3 2 1

Chronicle Books LLC
680 Second Street
San Francisco, California 94107
www.chroniclebooks.com

Tony Nourmand is co-owner of The Reel Poster Gallery in London, the premier international gallery for original, vintage film posters. He is author of *James Bond Movie Posters* and co-editor of a series of books with Graham Marsh on movie posters. He was Christie's London consultant for vintage film posters between 1992 and 2003.

Sir Christopher Frayling is Rector of London's Royal College of Art, where he is also Professor of Cultural History, and Chairman of Arts Council England. Historian, critic and award-winning broadcaster, he has written many books on film, popular culture and the arts.

Graham Marsh is an art director, illustrator and writer. He is the author and art director of many ground-breaking visual books, including *Blue Note Album Cover Art: The Ultimate Collection.*

June Marsh is a former fashion editor of the *Daily Mail, Country Life* and *Options.* She has written on fashion for the *Financial Times,* the *Telegraph,* the *Sunday Times* and the *Evening Standard.* She also lectures on fashion, and is involved in costume design for television.

Sarah Hodgson is an associate editor at Christie's and Head of the company's Popular Entertainment department in London. Since joining Christie's in 1993, she has handled, catalogued and sold hundreds of items of film memorabilia, and has co-authored a book on rock and pop music memorabilia.

Andreas Timmer is the president of TIMSON Media, Inc., a New York-based art consulting and media production company, and is the author of numerous essays on film posters. He holds an M.A. in art history from Brown University and a Ph.D. in film studies from Columbia University, and is the former curator of the Movie Poster Archive, New York.

AUDREY HEPBURN

THE PARAMOUNT YEARS

TONY NOURMAND

Foreword by Sir Christopher Frayling

CONTENTS

FOREWORD

2003 was the fiftieth anniversary of *Roman Holiday*, and just in case this had slipped the minds of visitors to the city, street markets all around the centre of Rome were crammed with postcards, lobby cards, posters, DVDs, records and calendars. Set-jetters camcorded themselves (this time round in colour) on all the main locations. William Wyler's film, which was 'photographed and recorded in its entirety in Rome, Italy' – as the 1953 credits proudly stated – had somehow come to embody the mass-media's love-affair with Rome in particular and Italy in general, a love-affair which began eight years after a devastating war. In the Mario Lanza film *The Seven Hills Of Rome* of a few years later, there's a helicopter tour of the city – to the strains of 'Arrivederci Roma' – during which Mario's friend Pepe takes a bird's-eye view which manages to include in its field of vision ancient history, Shakespeare and … *Roman Holiday* :

'The Roman Forum, that's where Julius Caesar was murdered. A little to the left Mark Antony made his famous speech. And over there by that broken column Audrey Hepburn fell asleep on Gregory Peck's shoulder.'

Wake up to a panoramic view of the city from the bedroom window of your palazzo; *meet* for an ice cream on the Spanish Steps; *motor* round the narrow streets on the back of a Vespa scooter, finishing up at the Colosseum; *place* your hand, cautiously, in the stone 'mouth of truth'; *party* the evening away on a barge by the Tiber; *eat* fettucini at Alfredo's on the Via della Scrofa – as Audrey Hepburn did while she was filming; and *at bedtime* back at the palazzo, try to say – with the halting rhythm, sing-song cadence and impeccable diction that in Cecil Beaton's celebrated phrase had a quality of heartbreak about it – 'Do you *know*, I've heard that there are people who sleep with *nothing* on!' *Roman Holiday* was made when Hollywood was moving onto the streets, tourism was picking up – though not yet in jets – and when in the headlines there was a real-life Buckingham Palace fairy tale involving the Queen's sister Princess Margaret and Group Captain Peter Townsend. One reason why the *Roman Holiday* revival is so very poignant, is that this story of a journalist (played by Gregory Peck) and a photographer (Eddie Albert), who decide in the end not to file a world exclusive about the private life of Princess Ann one day in Rome, can be seen again in a very different world where journalists and paparazzi chased Princess Diana into a tunnel one night in Paris. *Roman Holiday* has become if anything even more of a fairy tale over the past half century.

Audrey Hepburn played the Princess, and the part not only launched her, it began to turn her into a style icon. The credits, at Gregory Peck's specific request, equated the two names above the title by 'presenting Gregory Peck and introducing Audrey Hepburn'. It was as if this new star was a real princess from 'one of Europe's oldest ruling families' who had somehow smuggled herself into Hollywood. Many thought she was English. In fact, her father was an Anglo-Irish banker, her mother was a Dutch baroness and she was born in Belgium. Grace Kelly was soon to confirm her regal status by marrying a Prince who really *was* from one of Europe's oldest ruling families; Audrey Hepburn didn't need to. Her naïve grace – her quality of what one critic has called 'outrageous purity', combined with a dancer's movements and the kind of bone structure the camera loves – turned her into instant royalty. Most of her early films were variations on the Cinderella story.

'After so many drive-in waitresses becoming movie stars there has been this real drought, when along comes class, somebody who actually went to school, can spell, maybe even plays the piano. She may be a wispy, thin little thing, but when you see that girl you know you're really in the presence of something …'
William Wyler

RICHARD WINNINGTON (1905–1953) was an illustrator, caricaturist and strip cartoonist for the *News Chronicle*. He was also a left-wing journalist and film critic for this daily liberal paper. He produced this caricature for the *News Chronicle* UK issue of 21st August 1953.

Director William Wyler went some way towards explaining why, at the time:
'After so many drive-in waitresses becoming movie stars there has been this real drought, when along comes class, somebody who actually went to school, can spell, maybe even plays the piano. She may be a wispy, thin little thing, but when you see that girl you know you're really in the presence of something …'

Billy Wilder, who directed her second big film *Sabrina* the following year, was more blunt about it: 'She gave the distinct impression she could spell schizophrenia.'

Spell it, yes; experience it, never. Audrey Hepburn was as an actress always more famous for the outer person than the inner person. And where those drive-in waitresses were concerned, she was a whole world away from the sweater girls, sex kittens and blonde bombshells who presented their more obvious charms on the ever-widening screen. Jayne Mansfield parodied herself by clutching two bottles of milk to her ample bosom; Edith Head, meanwhile, said of Hepburn that she was all angles, like a Cubist painting – meaning the ideal figure for a costume designer to work with. *They* were in their natural habitat in Hollywood (Schwab's diner) or New York (the updraft from the subway); *she* was more at home in a Roman palazzo or at finishing school in Paris, or running down the steps with 'Winged Victory' behind her in the Louvre. Words like 'class', 'elegant', 'chic', 'poised' and 'elfin' soon became obligatory in reviews of her films.

In *Roman Holiday* audiences could see this new persona being created before their very eyes – as Audrey Hepburn had her hair cut short in gamine style, and as Eddie Albert's photographs of her awayday from royal duties were developed. Reminiscing about Stanley Donen's *Funny Face* (1957), Richard Avedon – the real-life model for fashion photographer Dick Avery (Fred Astaire) – once told me that his favourite scene in the film was when Astaire realizes just how beautiful Greenwich Village bookshop assistant Jo Stockton is, as his photographs of her – especially of her huge, heron-like eyes – are enlarged in the dark-room. Looking at the resulting images, Avery realizes that Jo doesn't, after all, have a funny face. Why he ever thought she did is anyone's guess. She was always covergirl material, and the best covers too. An ultra fashion plate.

But the transformation from *Funny Face* into the 'Audrey Hepburn look' wasn't just about fashion photography: it was also about Hubert de Givenchy who redesigned the look – broader eyebrows, raised dark hair, the contrast of dark and pale, geometry and strong shapes – to make it more grown-up and sophisticated. Givenchy once observed that Hepburn would make a potato sack look elegant, so his redesign had an excellent start. Which is why other style merchants such as Cecil Beaton and Noel Coward soon gravitated towards her orbit, why 'A' list directors – including Wyler, Wilder and Donen – wanted to work with her and why the finest still photographers in the business queued up to help enhance her public image. Beaton famously wrote of Audrey Hepburn's looks in *Vogue*, November 1954, that they were the perfect feminine ideal to emerge from the aftermath of the Second World War. They became so recognisable, in today's terms so iconic, that many if not most of the posters for Audrey Hepburn's films simply displayed those looks in the shop window. A few lines by the illustrator to suggest her structured features were enough. The most distinctive and celebrated poster image is of Hepburn as Holly Golightly – in Givenchy, pearls and diamonds, a ginger cat on her shoulder and a cigarette holder in her hand which could easily wrap around her waist, the most unlikely New York call-girl in the history of cinema. Truman Capote would have preferred the more credible Marilyn Monroe: he felt that the film version of *Breakfast At Tiffany's* gave too much sympathy, and far too much purity to the character of Holly. Someone should make that film one day. While we're waiting, who cares? Hepburn's kooky take on the part was the best comedy performance she ever gave, her New York was so much more stylish than

Opposite: After its American release, there was much hype around *Roman Holiday's* premiere worldwide. In Manila, Philippines, the film's premiere featured scooter riders circling the theatre with banners advertising its release.

anyone else's, and her thin, breathy version of 'Moon River' – which persuaded Henry Mancini that 'no one else has ever understood the song so completely' – sung while sitting on the fire escape of an East 71st Street apartment (and while giving Givenchy the day off, by wearing jeans and a pullover) was one of my Desert Island Discs. Not the souped-up harmonica and choral arrangement which was issued at the time, but her own recording. At times like these, Audrey Hepburn was a much better actress than the 'style' tag has given her credit for.

I wrote to her in the summer of 1991 at her home in Switzerland asking if she would agree to film a conversation for my 'cinema profiles' series on network television. She replied longhand, saying in a two-page letter how much the BBC had meant to her over the years and how delighted she would be, when next she was in London, to film a career interview with me for the series. But she died in January 1993, before it could happen. Her most recent appearance in a film – after a too-long absence – had been a cameo as a guardian angel in a long white knitted sweater, the gatekeeper of the after-life in Steven Spielberg's *Always* (1989). I'd certainly settle for that. As someone said, Dante himself never made paradise look quite so inviting.

CHRISTOPHER FRAYLING

INTRODUCTION

The seeds of this book were planted by Gordon Wise, the then head of the Boxtree imprint of Macmillan, in the summer of 2003. Gordon approached me to discuss the possibility of producing a book to celebrate the poster art of Audrey Hepburn's Paramount films. Although excited by the idea, when I analysed the scope of the available content it was apparent that to only include film posters would simply not provide sufficient material to justify a book. For this reason, I decided to include lobby cards, magazine covers and behind-the-scenes photographs to complement the poster imagery. Although I had encountered the various posters available for Hepburn's films, it was this wealth of photographic material that brought a new and exciting dimension to the project for me. The works of photographers like Bud Fraker, Bob Willoughby and Mark Shaw were a true inspiration and cast a revealing eye on Hepburn's career during her Paramount years. Together with the photography of Philippe Halsman, Norman Parkinson and Richard Avedon, they bring a fresh and light air to the rhythm of the book.

The posters that do exist for Hepburn's Paramount films are diverse and interesting and recruited the skills of international film-poster artists. In Italy, Ercole Brini's delicate watercolour style perfectly mirrored Hepburn's elegance. In America, renowned artist Robert McGinnis illustrated the most famous Hepburn campaign for *Breakfast At Tiffany's*. In Poland, Jerzy Flisak gave a characteristically quirky pop art edge to his design for *Roman Holiday*. In Japan, uncredited graphic artists were responsible for some of the most striking and uncluttered designs.

As the material was assembled, the theme of the book naturally gravitated towards the people who were responsible for creating the Hepburn image: the directors of her films, the costume designers, the photographers and the movie-poster artists. The images that these people created were the first encounter that the public had with Hepburn's screen persona.

In all my years as a vintage film poster dealer, not a day has gone by without an enquiry at the gallery about an Audrey Hepburn film poster. In fact, the first poster I ever managed to sell for a profit was the standard American poster for *Breakfast At Tiffany's*, back in 1989. More than Greta Garbo, Marlene Dietrich, Rita Hayworth, Bette Davis, Marilyn Monroe, Brigitte Bardot or any other female star – or male for that matter – Audrey Hepburn is by far the most collected film personality. Hepburn had a rare quality that is admired by both men and women. Her allure captivates women, who are never threatened by her beauty and grace and enthrals men, who are charmed by her vulnerability and elegance.

'Amid the rhinestone glitter of Roman Holiday's *make-believe, Paramount's new star sparkles and glows with the fire of a finely cut diamond.'*
Time *magazine*

Opposite: Hepburn stands beneath the Fulton Theater marquee that features her name over the title of the Broadway show *Gigi*, in which she played the leading role in January 1951. From here, she would go on to star in twenty feature films.

Perhaps the most quintessential and collectable Hepburn image is that which appears on the American poster for *Breakfast At Tiffany's*. With her long cigarette holder, Tiffany's diamond necklace, the iconic Givenchy black dress and a nameless cat upon her shoulder, Hepburn effortlessly commands one of the most enduring and timeless looks in cinematic history.

Two main people have played a significant part in helping to shape this book. The first is Graham Marsh, who came on board as art director and designer in March 2004. Having collaborated with Graham for over ten years, I was more than aware of his huge sensibility and knowledge of style and design and knew he was tailor-made for the project. Hepburn stood for simplicity and sophistication, which is exactly what Graham has delivered. The second person to whom I am equally indebted is Rebecca McClelland, who was introduced to me by my agent Leslie Gardner in July 2005. As my picture researcher, Rebecca opened my eyes to a whole new world of Hepburn imagery that I had never encountered. Her professionalism and commitment have been unconditional throughout.

In addition to Graham and Rebecca, I feel very fortunate to have had the involvement of the following respected and talented individuals, each of whom has contributed in a unique way to this publication.

I first met Christopher Frayling in 1995 soon after my friend and business partner, Bruce Marchant and I had opened The Reel Poster Gallery. One morning we arrived to find Christopher eagerly waiting for us to open up shop. He had come to see what material we had on the films of Sergio Leone – a personal passion and one on which he has written a number of books. Over the years, while Christopher acquires more titles before his name, our relationship has grown and I always get a kick out of my dealings with him. His contribution to this and other books I have had published is extremely valuable to me.

My collaboration with Sarah Hodgson began during my years as vintage film poster consultant for Christie's South Kensington. As Head of the Popular Entertainment Department, Sarah is extremely knowledgeable on collecting as a phenomenon. The first time she chose the cover for an auction catalogue was in 1996 and the image she chose was that of Audrey Hepburn on the standard American poster for *Breakfast At Tiffany's*. The poster sold for a record price of £8,625 / $13,800 (illustrated p. 95), a record which still stands today for this particular poster. Such shrewd decisions are typical of Sarah and over the years she has consistently judged the subtleties of the market with an expert's eye. She was the natural choice to contribute a piece to this book.

As the former curator of the Movie Poster Archive in New York, Andreas Timmer is someone I have encountered on many occasions. Incredibly thorough and professional, Andreas is passionate about film and art. He has always been gracious and generous with sharing valuable information that he has long researched. I was delighted when he expressed an interest in writing an innovative piece about Hepburn as a fashion icon.

As a prolific fashion editor, June Marsh is an encyclopaedia of fashion and has worked on numerous publications, including *Country Life*, the *Daily Telegraph* and the *Sunday Times*. I have known June as long as I have known Graham and could not have asked for anyone more equipped to write an informative essay offering a fresh look at Audrey Hepburn as a style icon.

Many of Hepburn's films, especially at Paramount Studios, centred on a fairy-tale theme. While Hepburn embraced these magical roles, the career path they paved was a fairy tale in itself. Likewise, since its humble conception, this publication took on a magical life of its own and has opened my eyes to the many faces of Audrey Hepburn. I hope you enjoy the book as much as I have enjoyed putting it together.

TONY NOURMAND

Opposite: 'Cat' elegantly poses with Hepburn who looks, as ever, perfectly dressed by Givenchy – dramatic costume jewellery, trademark cigarette holder and champagne being her only props. [Publicity shot on the set of *Breakfast At Tiffany's* (1961).]

ROMAN HOLIDAY (1953)

Starring

Joe Bradley	**GREGORY PECK**
Princess Ann	**AUDREY HEPBURN**
Irving Radovich	**EDDIE ALBERT**

Directed by	**WILLIAM WYLER**
Original Screenplay by	**IAN MCLELLAN HUNTER AND JOHN DIGHTON (BASED ON A STORY BY DALTON TRUMBO – UNCREDITED)**
Cinematography by	**HENRI ALEKAN AND FRANZ PLANER**
Costume Design by	**EDITH HEAD**

ACADEMY AWARD NOMINATIONS

EDDIE ALBERT
Best Actor in a Supporting Role

HAL PEREIRA AND WALTER H. TYLER
Best Art Direction / Set Decoration

FRANZ PLANER AND HENRI ALEKAN
Best Cinematography

WILLIAM WYLER
Best Director and Best Motion Picture

ROBERT SWINK
Best Film Editing

IAN MCLELLAN HUNTER AND JOHN DIGHTON
Best Writing / Screenplay

ACADEMY AWARDS WON

AUDREY HEPBURN
Best Actress in a Leading Role

EDITH HEAD
Best Costume Design

IAN MCLELLAN HUNTER
Best Writing / Motion Picture Story

DALTON TRUMBO (POSTHUMOUSLY IN 1993)
Best Writing / Motion Picture Story

ROMAN HOLIDAY

Roman Holiday is complete fantasy, offering an upside-down fairy-tale world where a disillusioned princess dreams of being a commoner for just one day. Fed up with her official duties and sheltered life, the young Princess Ann decides to run away. American journalist Joe Bradley discovers her sleeping on a bench and, soon realizing who she is, sees a once-in-a-lifetime opportunity to write a sensational story, uncovering the intimate secrets of the princess.

The princess innocently spends the night at Bradley's home. When she leaves his apartment he follows her and persuades her to spend the day with him to experience the freedom of enjoying the simple pleasures of life: a drink in a bar, a pixie haircut at the barber's and a dance by the river. At the dance, the secret services turn up and try to abduct her, but she escapes with Bradley. Once alone, they exchange a kiss but know it is time for her to return to the palace to perform her royal duties.

Unwilling to betray the princess, Bradley decides not to deliver his promised scoop to the newspaper. At the princess's press conference, Bradley and the princess say goodbye and his friend the photographer gives her a souvenir of photographs of their day, so that she will never forget the experience.

Unusually for its time, *Roman Holiday* was shot entirely on location in Rome. But ironically, the film's enchanting backdrop actually troubled director William Wyler, who deliberately shot the film in black and white so that the scenery would not outshine the story and characters. Rome's ancient quality provided an enchanting setting in which to introduce a fresh face to cinema audiences: Audrey Hepburn.

Wyler, who had not directed a non-dramatic motion picture since the 30s, had initially considered both Elizabeth Taylor and Jean Simmons for the leading role of the princess, but neither star was available. He therefore chose an unknown actress recommended by the French novelist Colette: Audrey Hepburn. Although she had already appeared in seven films, it was to be Hepburn's first starring role.

Hepburn's screen test took place at Pinewood Studios in London. As well as filming her acting out a few scenes from the script, her informal interview – during which she recalled memories of her wartime childhood – was also secretly recorded. The camera continued to roll and captured the moment of pure innocence when she became aware of the deception. The test reel was sent directly to Wyler in Rome, who found her enchanting and immediately knew that she was the one for the role. Hepburn and Willi, as he later became known, would become lifelong friends. Of Audrey Hepburn William Wyler said: 'In that league there's only ever been Garbo, and the other Hepburn, and maybe Bergman. It's a rare quality, but boy, do you know when you've found it.'

Roman Holiday was originally to be directed by Frank Capra in the 1940s, with Elizabeth Taylor and Cary Grant in the lead roles. However, a major obstacle blocked Capra's way: Paramount's policy of limiting film budgets to a ceiling of $1.5 million. As it stood, with Hepburn, Peck and Wyler, *Roman Holiday* was an instant hit when it opened in the summer of 1953 at New York's Radio City Music Hall.

French-born **WILLIAM WYLER** (1902–1981) began his extraordinary career at the young age of eighteen when Carl Laemmle, his mother's cousin – and head of Universal Studios – invited him to America to work in the publicity department at Universal. He worked his way up and just five years later made his directorial debut with *Crook Buster* (1925). He would go on to become one of the most highly regarded directors in the film world. Wyler had an ability to seek out the best in everyone he worked with and became famous for his numerous and laborious re-shootings of scenes. During his remarkable forty-five-year career, Wyler was nominated twelve times for the Best Director Oscar, winning three times: for *Mrs Miniver* in 1942, *The Best Years Of Our Lives* in 1946 and for *Ben-Hur* in 1959.

Opposite: Roman Holiday (1953)
US 41 x 27 in. (104 x 69 cm)
Courtesy of The Reel Poster Gallery

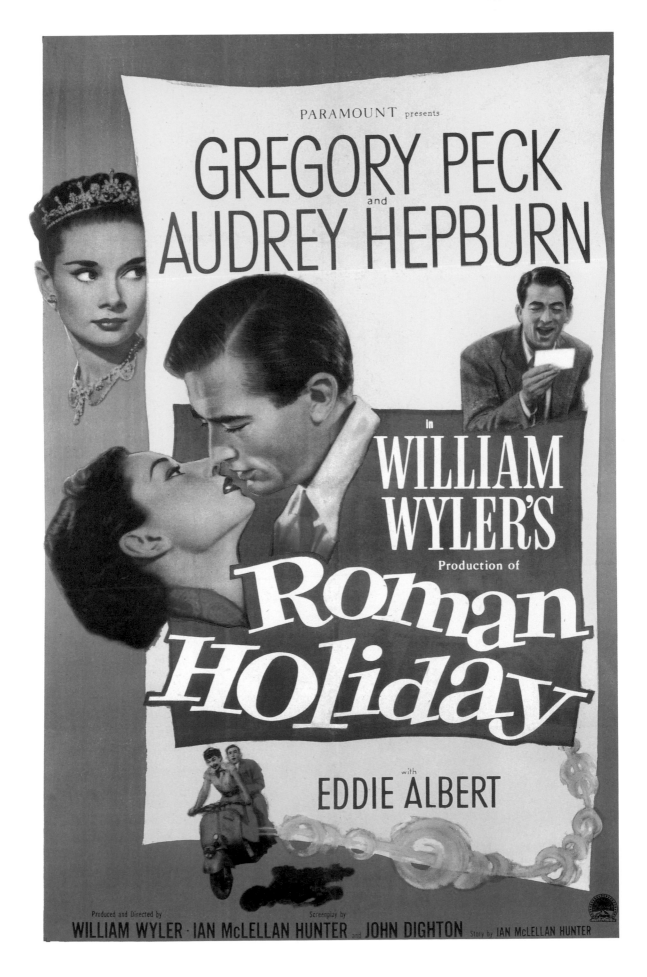

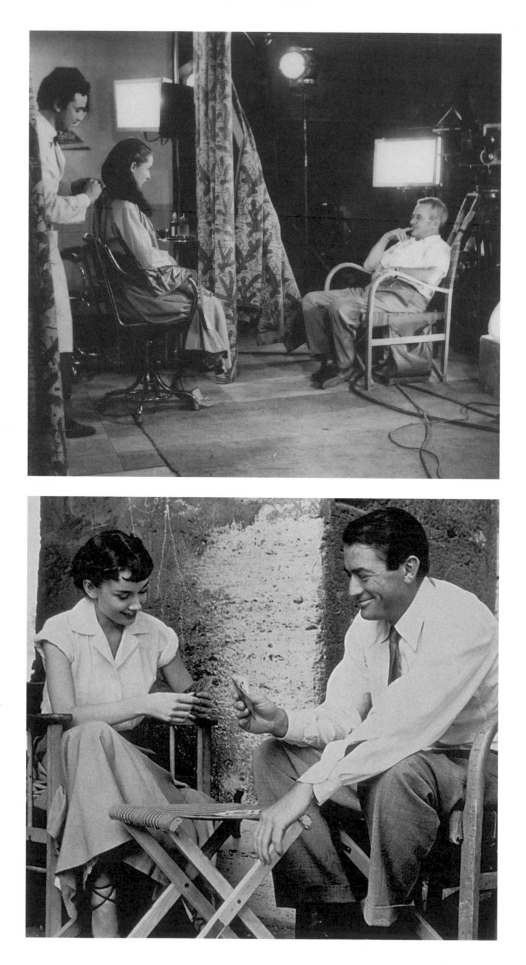

Above left: Wyler directs Hepburn discovering one of the simple joys of life – the freedom to choose her pixie haircut. *Left and opposite:* On location in Rome, a leisurely six-month shoot, where Hepburn and Peck had time to forge a lifelong friendship.

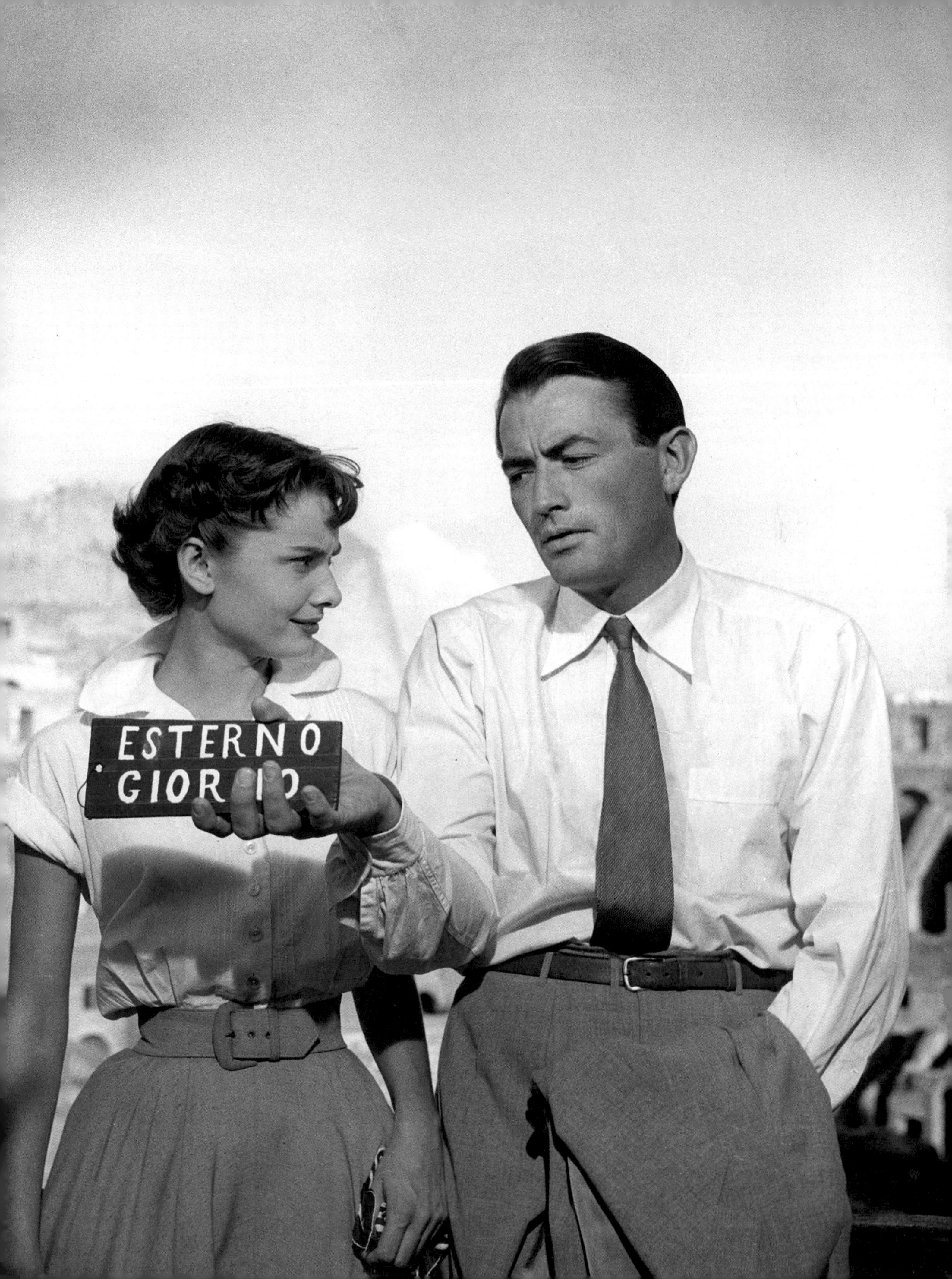
ESTERNO

Above: Roman Holiday (1953)
US 11 x 14 in. (28 x 36 cm)
No.1
Courtesy of The Reel Poster Gallery

Opposite: Roman Holiday (1953)
US 41 x 27 in. (104 x 69 cm)
(Re-release 1960)
Courtesy of The Reel Poster Gallery

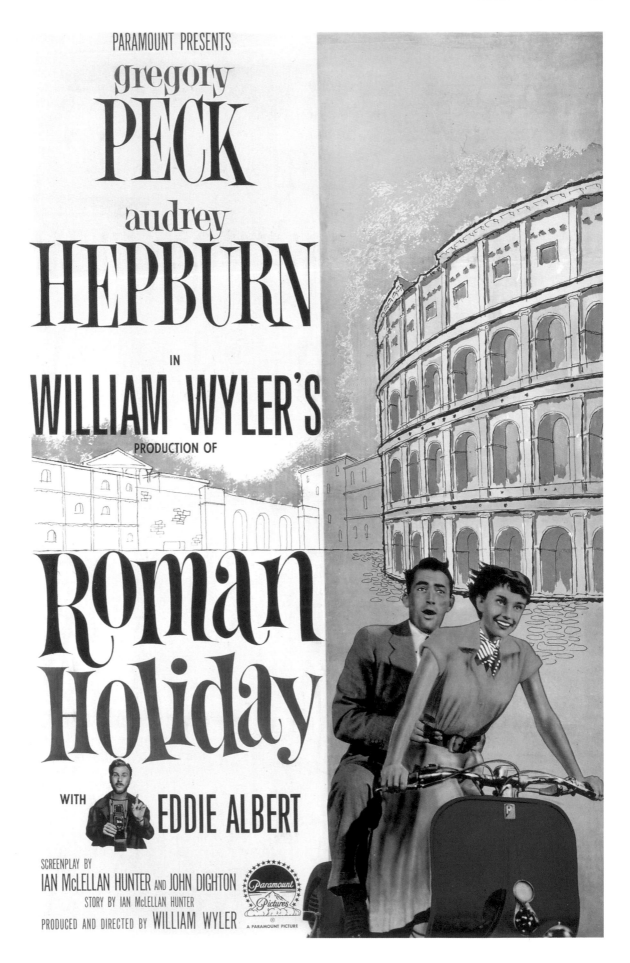

GREGORY PECK co-starred in Audrey Hepburn's debut film in 1953. Initially, director William Wyler had offered the part of Joe Bradley to Cary Grant, who recognized immediately that Hepburn would be the main focus of the film and so declined the role. The part was graciously accepted by Gregory Peck. His strong but gentle personality enabled Hepburn to be at ease, creating a breathtaking on-screen chemistry between the two. Whilst working with the unknown Hepburn, Peck quickly realized that she would become a huge star and told Wyler that her name should be moved up higher on the order of credits. He knew that she would win an Oscar for her performance and wanted to prevent an embarrassing situation later. Gregory Peck (1916–2003) was born in La Jolla, California. In 1939 he enrolled in the Neighborhood Playhouse in New York and made his debut on Broadway in *The Morning Star* (1942). By 1943 he was in Hollywood and cast in the RKO film *Days Of Glory*. But it was his performance in *The Keys Of The Kingdom* that elevated him to star status when he was nominated for an Academy Award. Peck's screen presence displayed the qualities for which he became well known – tall, handsome, heroic and noble. He appeared in Hitchcock's *Spellbound* in 1945 and in *The Yearling*, for which he was again nominated for an Academy Award and won a Golden Globe in 1946. With a string of hits behind him and after four nominations, in 1962 Peck finally won the Oscar for his performance as lawyer Atticus Finch in *To Kill A Mockingbird*. In later life Peck made a comeback with films such as *The Omen* (1976), *MacArthur* (1977) and *The Boys From Brazil* (1978). He received the Academy's 'Jean Hersholt Humanitarian Award' and the Presidential Medal of Freedom, America's highest civilian award.

*Opposite: Roman Holiday
(Vacanze Romane) (1953)*
Italian 55 x 39 in. (140 x 99 cm)
Art by Franco Fiorenzi
Courtesy of Yoshitaka Miyamoto

Born in Rome, **ERCOLE BRINI** (1913–1989) studied at that city's famous Accademia di Belle Arti. During the Second World War he began to focus solely on cinematographic art, for which he became renowned. During the 50s, he was the principal artist for Paramount Studios in Italy and produced designs for the five Hepburn titles featured in this book, which are among some of the most sought-after film posters today. A key member of a sparkling generation of post-war Italian film-poster artists, Brini was known for his distinctive watercolour style that often revealed the emotional content of the film. Touching on a wide array of genres from drama, film noir and thrillers to Italian neo-realism, musicals and romantic comedies, he produced the artwork for classics such as *Bicycle Thieves* (1948 – released in the US as *The Bicycle Thief*), *Sunset Boulevard* (1950), *Miracle In Milan* (1951), *To Catch A Thief* (1955), *Breakfast At Tiffany's* (1961) and *Blow-Up* (1966).

Opposite: Roman Holiday
(Vacanze Romane) (1953)
Italian 79 x 55 in. (201 x 140 cm)
Art by Ercole Brini
Courtesy of Kiyoshi Ozeki

Above: Roman Holiday (Vacanze Romane) (1953)
All Italian 19 x 13 in. (48 x 33 cm)
From left to right: Courtesy of The Reel Poster
Gallery, Courtesy of the Stephen Coller
Collection, Courtesy of the Haruhisa
Minekawa Collection.
Opposite: Italian 27 x 19 in. (69 x 48 cm)
Courtesy of The Reel Poster Gallery

Audrey Hepburn's famous gamine style was engineered by internationally acclaimed costume designer **EDITH HEAD** (1897–1981). In 1932 she applied for a job at Paramount Studios as a sketch artist and was taken on despite her lack of experience. With time, she began to be trusted with the up-and-coming stars and in 1938 she became head designer. Despite her tough character, Head was very comfortable dealing with the stars, always making them feel all-important. Consequently, they would repeatedly ask for her to dress them. She developed a good working relationship with Elizabeth Taylor and won an Oscar for her costume design for Taylor in *A Place In The Sun* (1951). She also worked extensively with Alfred Hitchcock, designing Grace Kelly's wardrobe for *Rear Window* (1954) and *To Catch A Thief* (1955). During her prolific sixty-year career, Edith Head was nominated thirty-five times for the Best Costume Design Oscar and won eight. Her abilities extended to a keen sense of self-promotion, making her the most famous film costume designer of all time.

Above left: Original Edith Head costume sketch for *Roman Holiday* (1953); *above centre and right:* for *Sabrina* (1954).
Opposite: Hepburn meets Edith Head during her first photo shoot at Paramount (1953). Photo by Bob Willoughby.

Above: Roman Holiday
(Rzymskie Wakacje) (1953)
Polish 33 x 23 in. (84 x 58 cm)
Art by Jerzy Flisak

JERZY FLISAK was born in 1930 in Poznan, Poland. Graduating from the Institute of Architecture in Warsaw in 1953, he went on to become one of Poland's most admired graphic artists. His designs were used for several book and magazine covers while his satirical cartoons featured in magazines such as *Szpilki*. From the early 60s to the mid 70s he designed film posters, most notably for *Playtime* (1967), *The Little Prince* (1974), *The Conversation* (1974) and *Young Frankenstein* (1974). He has exhibited worldwide from Canada to Berlin and won a number of awards, including the Art Directors' Club of New York Award for his 1962 poster 'Najemny Morderca' for the Italian film *Il Sicario* (*The Hit Man*).

Under the Soviet regime, **BORIS CHALIAPIN** (1904–1979) undertook a programme to study art and sculpture. He was the son of the renowned Russian opera singer Fyodor Chaliapin, who was often the subject of Boris's portraits. In 1925 Chaliapin moved to Paris, and held his first exhibition two years later in the foyer of the London Covent Garden Theatre. His career took off following a chance encounter with a former foreign news editor of *Time* magazine. In 1939 he was commissioned to illustrate his first magazine cover for *Time*, featuring the Indian political leader Jawaharlal Nehru. This was to be the first of 400 covers that he would come to illustrate over the next three decades. Chaliapin was part of the famous ABC (Artzybasheff, Baker, Chaliapin) trio of *Time* illustrators who, for some twenty-eight years, were responsible for over fifty per cent of the magazine's covers.

Opposite: Time magazine, September 7th 1953.
Cover art by Boris Chaliapin.

TWENTY CENTS

SEPTEMBER 7, 1953

TIME

THE WEEKLY NEWSMAGAZINE

Boris Chaliapin

AUDREY HEPBURN

Behind the sparkle of rhinestones, a diamond's glow.

$6.00 A YEAR

(REG. U.S. PAT. OFF.)

VOL. LXII NO. 10

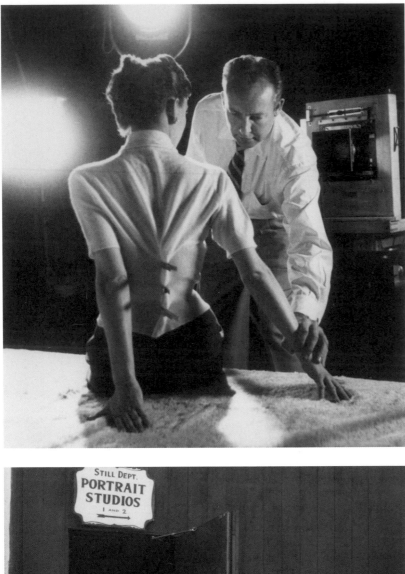

BUD FRAKER (1916–2002) was born in Altoona, Pennsylvania. In 1934 he studied photography at Los Angeles City College and began working part-time at the Columbia Studios stills laboratory under his brother William 'Bill' Fraker, who was director of the department. Following Bill's death, Fraker was hired by Hollywood photographer A. L. 'Whitey' Schafer at Columbia. By the time he left Columbia in 1942, Bud was head of publicity photography at the studio. In 1942 Fraker followed Schafer to Paramount, where he became responsible for the Publicity Photography Department and assisted in the portrait gallery. Upon Schafer's death, Fraker took over as director of stills photography at Paramount. It was during this period that he encountered Paramount's new star Audrey Hepburn for the first time and photographed her to promote *Roman Holiday*. Fraker continued to work at Paramount until the 1960s, when he left to run his own photography lab and freelance for other film studios.

Above left: Cinching in Hepburn's sweater with wooden clothes-pegs for a closer fit, photographer Bud Fraker prepares Hepburn for a publicity shot for *Roman Holiday*.
Below left: After her portrait sitting, Hepburn leaves the studio and, assisted by Bud Fraker, carries clothes back to her car.
Opposite: Bud Fraker sets up a portrait shot of Hepburn.
All photos by Bob Willoughby.

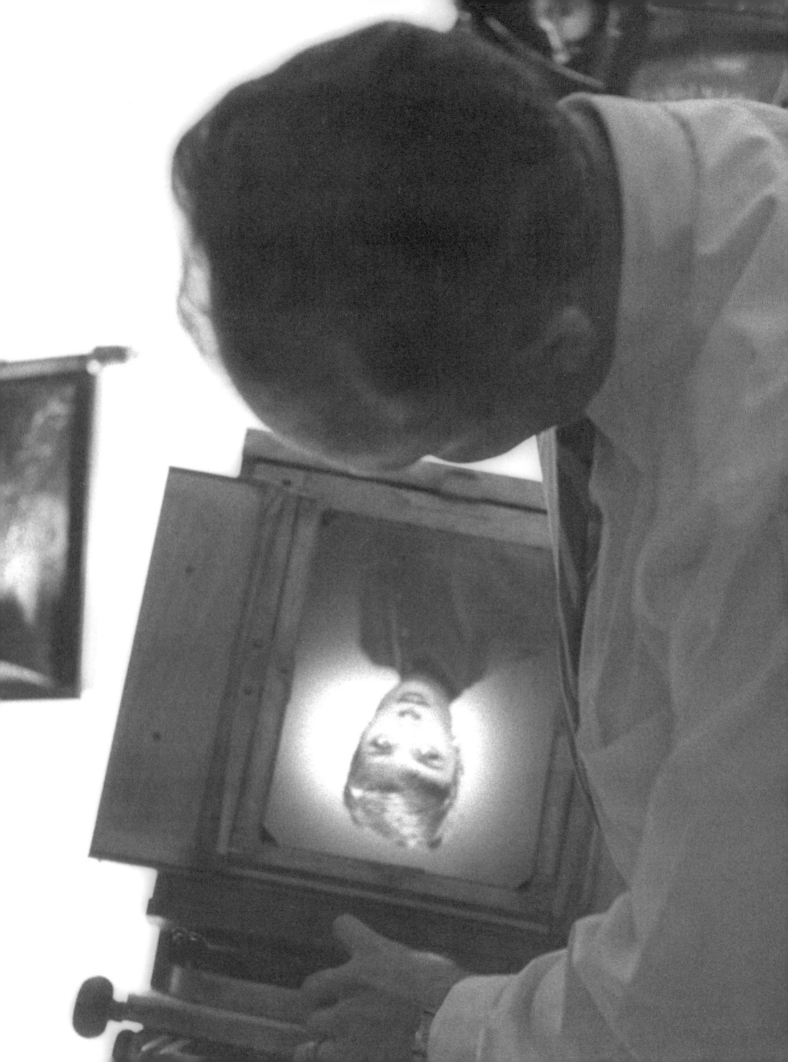

Sensuous, funny and oh so sleepy, Hepburn poses in the voluminous nightgown she wore as Princess Ann in *Roman Holiday*. *Above left:* Photo by Bob Willoughby. *Above and Opposite:* Photos by Bud Fraker.

Above: Hepburn overwhelmed by the paparazzi after receiving her Academy Award for *Roman Holiday*.
Opposite: Leonard McCombe's lens flare gives a dreamlike quality to this shot of Hepburn holding her Academy Award.

SABRINA (1954)

Starring

Sabrina Fairchild	AUDREY HEPBURN
Linus Larrabee	HUMPHREY BOGART
David Larrabee	WILLIAM HOLDEN

Directed by	BILLY WILDER
Original Screenplay by	ERNEST LEHMAN, BILLY WILDER AND SAMUEL A. TAYLOR
Cinematography by	CHARLES LANG
Costume Design by	EDITH HEAD AND HUBERT DE GIVENCHY (UNCREDITED)

ACADEMY AWARD NOMINATIONS

AUDREY HEPBURN
Best Actress in a Leading role

HAL PEREIRA, WALTER H. TYLER, SAM COMER AND RAY MOYER
Best Art Direction / Set Decoration

CHARLES LANG
Best Cinematography

BILLY WILDER
Best Director

ERNEST LEHMAN, BILLY WILDER AND SAMUEL A. TAYLOR
Best Writing / Screenplay

ACADEMY AWARDS WON

EDITH HEAD
Best Costume Design

SABRINA

A light-hearted romantic drama, *Sabrina* is the story of the shy daughter of a chauffeur who lives on a large estate belonging to the Larrabee family on Long Island. Living amongst the servants in this 'upstairs, downstairs' household, she falls for David, the playboy son of the house, who does not know of her existence. Sabrina's father sends her away to Paris to attend a cookery school, but her experience teaches her more than just how to cook. She graduates and returns a beautiful and sophisticated woman – and immediately catches David's eye. Unfortunately David is already engaged to another woman, who would provide a very profitable arrangement for his family business. His older brother and business partner Linus decides to distract Sabrina from David so that the marriage goes ahead and the business prospects remain good. Linus wines and dines the naïve Sabrina with the intention of eventually sending her away to live, all expenses paid, in Paris. But as he spends time with her, they fall in love. Linus tries to fight his unexpected feelings but then gives in and they leave together bound for Paris.

Following Hepburn's Oscar-winning performance in *Roman Holiday,* huge anticipation surrounded the filming of her second Hollywood film. The combined efforts of Academy Award winners Billy Wilder, William Holden, Humphrey Bogart and Audrey Hepburn resulted in a film that became a big hit at the box office. Earning Paramount substantial profits, *Sabrina* was both critically and publicly admired.

The filming took just seven weeks on a set on Long Island and at Paramount Studios, with a budget of just over $2 million. Paramount were happy to capitalize on Hepburn's success while still paying her only $15,000 to play the starring role, whilst her co-stars William Holden and Humphrey Bogart commanded $150,000 and $300,000 respectively. During the production of *Sabrina,* Wilder continually worked on the script, even reportedly asking Hepburn on one occasion to feign illness to give him more time. The role of Linus had been intended for Cary Grant, but when the actor dropped out a week before filming, Wilder approached Humphrey Bogart. Although he accepted, Bogart disapproved of Hepburn playing the part of Sabrina and would have preferred his wife Lauren Bacall for the role. Perhaps this accounts for an underlying lack of chemistry between on-screen lovers Linus and Sabrina. In contrast, William Holden and Hepburn fell in love during the shoot. Hepburn's youthful innocence and vulnerability made her perfectly suited for the part as the shy young Sabrina. But she also had the elegance and poise to carry off the character's transformation into a lady of absolute sophistication. Wilder in particular appreciated Hepburn's reliability as an actress who would always have her lines prepared. He would comment that although she had never been to acting school, she made her performance look easy through pure hard work and a very natural ability. They worked together again on *Love In The Afternoon* in 1957.

Although Edith Head won the Oscar for best costume design, the uncredited Hubert de Givenchy was responsible for many of Hepburn's outfits in the film. Recalling his first encounter with Miss Hepburn, Givenchy noted that he had been expecting the glamorous Katharine Hepburn to walk in, but was instead faced with a very different creature. Taken aback by the beauty of her eyes and her slenderness, nonetheless at first he did not think he could design for her. But a very bold Hepburn knew exactly how she wanted to look, and asked to view his latest collection. With Givenchy's expertise, together they created the easily accessible Audrey Hepburn style.

Polish-born **BILLY WILDER** (1906–2002) began his film career in 1929 as a screenwriter in Berlin. On Hitler's rise to power in 1933, Wilder realized that his Jewish ancestry put him in danger and so immediately fled to Paris and in turn to the US. Despite the language barrier and with the help of his flatmate actor Peter Lorre, he managed to break through into the American film industry. In 1938 he began writing with Charles Brackett. Their producer-director partnership would go on to create titles such as *Double Indemnity* (1944), *The Lost Weekend* (1945) – for which Wilder won an Oscar for Best Director – and *Sunset Boulevard* (1950). During his fifty-year career he was nominated for eight Best Director Academy Awards in all, second only to William Wyler. Wilder's filmography boasts classics such as *The Seven Year Itch* (1955), *Some Like It Hot* (1959) and *The Apartment* (1960), for which he won his second Oscar for Best Director. His work appealed to both mainstream audiences and tough critics alike. He retired in 1981.

Opposite: Sabrina (1954)
US 41 x 27 in. (104 x 69 cm)

HUMPHREY BOGART
AUDREY HEPBURN
WILLIAM HOLDEN

"SABRINA"

with
WALTER HAMPDEN · JOHN WILLIAMS · MARTHA HYER · JOAN VOHS

PRODUCED AND DIRECTED BY
BILLY WILDER

Written for the Screen by BILLY WILDER, SAMUEL TAYLOR and ERNEST LEHMAN
From the play by SAMUEL TAYLOR   A PARAMOUNT PICTURE

THREE ACADEMY AWARD STARS IN THEIR GREATEST ROLES

HUMPHREY BOGART (1899–1957) was born in New York on Christmas Day. In 1918 he enlisted in the US Navy and was assigned to the USS *Leviathan*. It has been rumoured that this is where he acquired the famous scar on his lip. In the early 1920s he managed a theatre company and it was not long before he was acting himself. Following a series of stage appearances and minor film parts, his breakthrough role came in 1936 as an escaped killer in *The Petrified Forest*. Contracted to Warner Brothers, from 1936 to 1940 he starred in a staggering twenty-eight films. However, he became increasingly bored by a steady stream of parts playing criminals or gangsters, and soon craved more diverse roles.

In 1941 Bogart played two of his most memorable characters: Roy 'Mad Dog' Earle in *High Sierra*, and a pitch-perfect Sam Spade in *The Maltese Falcon*. 1943 marked the peak of his career. Starring opposite Ingrid Bergman, Bogart played Rick Blaine in the romantic war drama *Casablanca*. Warner Brothers were responsible for bringing Bogart and his fourth wife together. In an adaptation of Ernest Hemingway's novel *To Have And Have Not* (1944), Bogart was paired up with twenty-year-old actress Betty Perske, whose stage name was Lauren Bacall. The chemistry between the two was incredible and they were married just one year later. Bogart went on to make a number of classic films including *The Big Sleep* (1946), *Key Largo* (1948) and *The African Queen* (1951), the latter for which he won his only Oscar. *Sabrina* was one of the last of the almost eighty movies of Bogart's career.

Above left: Comparing notes with co-star William Holden. *Below left:* Hepburn dances barefoot with Billy Wilder. *Opposite:* Cycling on the set with co-star Humphrey Bogart.

Left: While Hepburn perches on a narrow step on the set of *Sabrina*, Billy Wilder lends a hand.

Opposite: Sabrina (1954)
Italian 79 x 55 in. (201 x 140 cm)
Art by Ercole Brini

Above: Sabrina (1954)
Japanese 30 x 20 in. (76 x 51 cm)
(Re-release 1965)
Courtesy of The Reel Poster Gallery

Opposite: French poodles unsuccessfully
attempt to steal the limelight, whilst
Hepburn poses for a *Sabrina* publicity shot.

Above: Sabrina (1954)
Polish 33 x 23 in. (84 x 58 cm)
Art by Maciej Żbikowski

MACIEJ ŻBIKOWSKI (b. 1935) was born in Przasnysz, Poland. Żbikowski studied glassmaking at WSRA in Wroclaw and graphic design at Warsaw ASP, where he graduated in 1960. He then worked in an animation studio, producing satirical cartoons and drawings, which would feature in weekly magazines such as *Szpilki* and *Polska*. Many of these images have since been exhibited in Poland, Russia, Germany, China and Vietnam. In the 1960s and 1970s he designed numerous film posters for the later Polish releases of *Red River* (1948), *Deadline U.S.A.* (1952), *Sabrina* (1954) and *The Graduate* (1967). As a cartoonist, he produced simple, bold and bright images that would often offer an abstract representation of these American films.

Opposite: Sabrina (1954)
Spanish 39 x 27 in. (99 x 69 cm)
Art by Fernando Albericio

Hepburn was visited on the set of *Sabrina* by a host of Hollywood personalities. *From top:* Dean Martin and Jerry Lewis; George Marshall, and a studio executive; Rosemary Clooney; Danny Kaye and Bing Crosby. *Opposite:* Marlene Dietrich. Photos by Bob Willoughby.

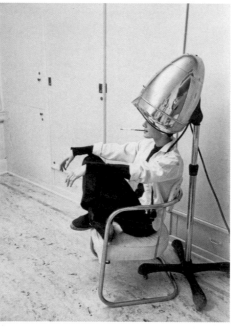

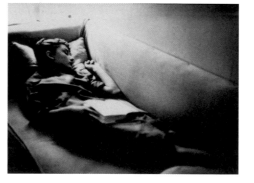

American photographer **MARK SHAW** (1922–1969) travelled extensively during his career. At the age of thirty he started working as a photographer for numerous magazines including *Harper's Bazaar*, *Mademoiselle* and *Life*. During his sixteen years with *Life* magazine, he shot twenty-seven covers and provided images for almost 100 stories. Shaw was also one of the first fashion photographers permitted to shoot behind the scenes and on the catwalks at couture shows, but his work was not confined to the world of fashion. His photographs of the rich and famous range from Pablo Picasso, Brigitte Bardot and Elizabeth Taylor to Pope Paul VI, Grace Kelly, Yves Saint Laurent and Audrey Hepburn. He is perhaps most noted for his work between 1959 and 1963 when he took family photographs of President John F. Kennedy, his wife Jackie and their children. By not intruding or breaking boundaries of intimacy, Shaw gained their trust and formed a special relationship with the family. He documented the most tender moments of their lives, such as the birth of their child John-John. Towards the end of his career, Shaw won numerous awards for his still photography and for his later work filming television commercials.

Above: In 1953 Mark Shaw photographed Hepburn on the set of *Sabrina* for a two-page feature in *Life* magazine dedicated to Hepburn's daily life.
Opposite: Hepburn having fun with Mark Shaw on the set of *Sabrina*.

Born and educated in New York City, **DENNIS STOCK** (b. 1928) began his photographic journey as the apprentice to *Life* magazine photographer Gjon Mili. Stock won first prize in *Life* magazine's Young Photographers Contest in 1951 and subsequently became associated with the world-renowned agency, Magnum Photos. His unique talent lies in his ability to spot the shot that summarizes a situation or epitomises a personality. His pure open-mindedness and refined technical skills have produced exceptional compositions and iconic images. Most are portraits, of either known or unknown subjects. But all are taken in the subjects' environment: James Dean reciting his favourite poet, James Whitcomb Riley in his uncle's Winslow Farm in Fairmount, hippies on the Berkeley campus, sunbathers at the McCoy Commune in Novato or Audrey Hepburn in the back seat of her studio car. From 1957 to 1960 his spirited shots of the US jazz and blues scene captured musicians like Louis 'Satchmo' Armstrong, Billie Holiday, Miles Davis and Duke Ellington fully absorbed in their art. These won Stock first prize in the International Photography Competition in Poland in 1962 and were published as a volume, *Jazz Street*. Until the 80s Stock kept to the tradition of black-and-white reportage, primarily for editorial outlets. But his imagery was by no means limited to documenting the lives of the charismatic and famous. In the late 60s he undertook on-the-road projects that gave an authentic insight into subjects such as the Hell's Angels and hippy alternative living. Stock has run numerous workshops and lectured widely across Europe and the United States. His work has been internationally exhibited and his photographs have been acquired by most major museum collections.

Left: On the set of *Sabrina*, Hepburn's healthy appetite belied the slender frame and tiny waistline that made it possible for her to wrap and tie a shirt into a knot at the back. *Opposite:* Captured deep in thought in the back of her studio car.
Photos by Dennis Stock.

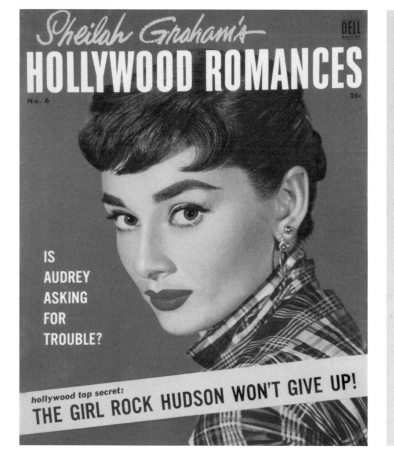

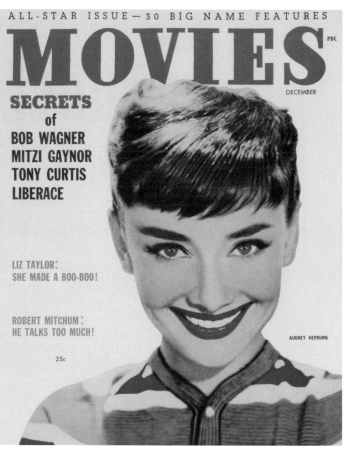

Above: Sheilah Graham's *Hollywood Romances* and *Movies,* both from December 1954. *Opposite:* Publicity shot for the film's Christmas release.

COLLECTING AUDREY
WHAT PRICE FAME?

Admiring someone is one thing; purchasing memorabilia associated with them is quite another. The reasons an individual might want to do this can only be speculated about, but essentially, in making the acquisition one is buying into that person, and there is clearly a desire to have a closer association.

Audrey Hepburn, as has been suggested in the foreword to this book, arouses feelings of admiration, desire, aspiration even, and in recent years collectors and those with no collecting history whatsoever have been buying into her in increasing numbers, paying ever higher prices for a piece of her, whether it be a film poster, a signed photograph, a letter, or perhaps most coveted of all, one of her memorable costumes. For many she will always be Holly Golightly and anything associated with *Breakfast At Tiffany's* seems to be what is most sought after, reflected best in the prices paid for posters for the film. In 2004, Christie's sold a rare, special style, double-sided US one-sheet poster bearing the classic image of Hepburn with cat and cigarette holder, wearing the Givenchy gown, for £13,145 ($23,500 – illus. p. 101). With an estimated value of £4,000–£6,000, this was a record for any Hepburn poster at auction. This had been preceded no fewer than eight years earlier in 1996 by a standard US one-sheet selling for £8,625 ($13,800 – illus. p. 95). Variations in size with the same image appear regularly at auction and command upwards of £2,000. As a general rule it is the US posters that are most in demand for her films, but in 1999, Christie's sold the Italian poster for *Sabrina* – estimated at £1,600–£2,400, with artwork by Ercole Brini – for £9,775 ($16,130 – illus. p. 45). Similarly, non-American posters for *Breakfast At Tiffany's* have often realized prices well above their estimates. The British quad poster sold in 2001 for £1,998 ($3,520); in 2004 the German poster sold for £1,135 ($2,050) and in the same year the Danish rendition realized £1,792 ($3,225).

In the twenty or so years that the market for film memorabilia has really taken off, very few costumes or personal effects have been offered at auction, but what has been sold, and the prices achieved, illustrates the demand. At Christie's New York in 1996, the diamante hair ornament worn by Hepburn for the publicity photos and posters for *Breakfast At Tiffany's* realized $17,825 (£11,355). The provenance of such pieces is crucial and in this instance the item had been given to the vendor in 1964 by the costume designer Edith Head. At Christie's London in 2000, the two-piece raspberry bouclé wool suit designed by Givenchy, worn by Hepburn in the scene where she strolls along the river Seine in Paris with Cary Grant in *Charade*, sold for £7,637 ($11,990).

Opposite: Hepburn in evening dress for the opening scene of *Breakfast At Tiffany's* wearing the long silk duchesse gown by Givenchy and the diamante hair ornament that realized $17,825 (£11,355) at auction in 1996.

More recently, in 2004, one of her most memorable costumes from *My Fair Lady* was included at auction in the US. Cecil Beaton's striking designs for the Ascot racing scenes are a key part of the film, and Hepburn's black and white creation was offered with a breathtaking estimate of $100,000–$150,000. It sold for $100,000. In the same sale Beaton's original costume design sold for $25,000. This begs the question: what, in the unlikely event of it ever being offered at auction, would the signature black Givenchy dress worn in *Breakfast At Tiffany's* realize? The answer will be revealed at an auction at Christie's in London in December 2006. Three dresses were made for the memorable opening sequence; one is in the Museum of Costume in Madrid, one is in the archives at Maison Givenchy and the third was retained by Hepburn after filming and subsequently returned to Hubert de Givenchy, who has donated it for auction to support the work of Dominique Lapierre's *City Of Joy Aid* in India.

In 1998, a fascinating collection of correspondence and family photographs were consigned to Christie's by Hepburn's stepmother, Fidelma Hepburn-Ruston. Seen for the first time by anyone outside the family, the collection gave a unique insight into Hepburn's complex relationship with her father, and her absolute love and devotion to her family, especially her sons. The letters show glimpses of the very human side of the screen star, as she discusses juggling the demands of work with her role as wife and mother. The correspondence spanned several decades from the 1960s to the 1990s and touches on some significant moments. Very often the letters and notes are signed affectionately with the initials of her father's nickname for her, 'Monkey Puzzle'. (According to her stepmother, Hepburn's father had found her mischievous as a child and sometimes difficult to understand.)

The collection was divided into two lots: one comprising approximately sixty-four family snap-shots, publicity portraits and stills from 1939–1989, which realized £24,150 ($41,055); the other lot comprised the correspondence, eleven letters and five assorted postcards and greetings cards, which realized £45,500 ($77,350). The results should perhaps speak for themselves.

A few years later, in December 2004, two further letters from the same collection emerged. One, written to her father in March 1963, refers to their long estrangement, and her shock at learning that the grandmother whom she 'adored' had given an interview about her to an Austrian newspaper: '… I was terribly shocked, to be somehow commercialized by my own grandmother at a time when I desperately wanted to be loved for myself…' The second letter, sent to her stepmother over twenty years later, expresses similar feelings with regard to a book: '… an unauthorized "biography" of me. Two such books have been written both without my cooperation and permission, nor have I read them as I am disgusted by such an invasion of privacy, naturally also inaccurate as they can only write from hearsay…' (Sold for £1,314 / $2240.)

A smaller item from the same collection, but one with important family connections for Hepburn, was a 30s silver and enamel powder compact. It was originally a gift to Hepburn from her grandmother, and in turn was given many years later by Audrey to her stepmother. Its value as a pretty vintage piece would be in the region of £50–£60 ($85–$105); because it had belonged to Hepburn, its value climbed to over £1,700 ($2,890).

Doubtless there are other examples of Hepburn memorabilia being bought and sold, but what the above shows is that her popularity has grown significantly in recent years, and there is no reason to doubt that it will continue to do so.

Opposite: An original costume sketch by Edith Head for *Funny Face*. Courtesy of The Reel Poster Gallery

SARAH HODGSON

FUNNY FACE (1957)

Starring

Jo Stockton	**AUDREY HEPBURN**
Dick Avery	**FRED ASTAIRE**
Maggie Prescott	**KAY THOMPSON**

Directed by	**STANLEY DONEN**
Original Screenplay by	**LEONARD GERSHE**
Cinematography by	**RAY JUNE**
Costume Design by	**HUBERT DE GIVENCHY**
	AND EDITH HEAD
Special Visual Consultant and Main Title Backgrounds by	**RICHARD AVEDON**

ACADEMY AWARD NOMINATIONS

HAL PEREIRA, GEORGE W. DAVIS, SAM COMER AND RAY MOYER
Best Art Direction / Set Decoration

RAY JUNE
Best Cinematography

HUBERT DE GIVENCHY AND EDITH HEAD
Best Costume Design

LEONARD GERSHE
Best Writing / Story and Screenplay Written Directly
for the Screen

FUNNY FACE

By 1957 Hepburn commanded above-the-title billing with Fred Astaire in a musical that would demonstrate her training as a dancer. Hepburn was cast as Jo Stockton, an intellectual Greenwich Village bookstore clerk who is discovered by fashion photographer Dick Avery (played by Astaire and based on real-life photographer Richard Avedon). With the help of a promised trip to Paris – where Jo would be able to meet Professor Emile Flostre, whose philosophy of 'empathicalism' she has keenly followed for years – Dick persuades Jo to put aside her highbrow principles and become *Quality* magazine's 'Woman of the Year'. While photographing her in Paris, a romance develops between them. Punctuated by memorable Gershwin tunes, energetic dance sequences, vibrant colour schemes and multiple couture extravaganzas, *Funny Face* both glamorized and satirized the fashion industry. Perhaps more than any other Hepburn movie, it is a blatant fashion statement.

This was Hepburn's first musical and she demonstrated her singing abilities by performing all her own songs. The plot is based on Leonard Gershe's Broadway musical *Wedding Bells*. The film's unique look and colour composition was largely due to the vision of Richard Avedon who was responsible for most of the photography in the film, including the famous facial portrait of Hepburn unveiled during the dark-room sequence.

Hepburn confessed how frightened she was at her first meeting with Fred Astaire:

'I'll never forget the morning I was to meet Fred for the first time. We were to begin rehearsals at the studio in Hollywood, and I remember being so shaken that I threw up my breakfast. Stanley [Donen], himself having been a dancer, was remarkably encouraging, but on that particular day I was so ready to crumble that no words of comfort from anyone could have sufficed. And Fred, perhaps, was nervous too, over how he was going to get on with me. Well, unlucky fellow, he had every right to worry, because sure enough, as soon as we started on the rehearsal stage, the worst that could have happened did. I was tripping all over Fred's feet. I could barely walk, let alone dance with him. I'm sure he and Stanley were silently thinking to themselves: My God, what are we going to do with this clumsy girl? But if they did, they never let me in on it. Fred, always the gentleman, only said, "That's marvellous, but let's try it again." And so we did. (It was a tiny bit better that time.) And again. (Better still, but nowhere up to his standard, I could tell.) And again, until finally, long hours later, under the quiet, ever watchful eye of Stanley and Fred himself, I was dancing with Fred Astaire. Imagine – dancing with Fred Astaire!'

Rainy Parisian weather played havoc with the shooting of the wedding dress dance scene. Slipping in the muddy grass, both Hepburn and Astaire's dancing skills were challenged by the wet conditions. Filming the Parisian scenes was also stressful due to the riots and political upheaval that gripped the city at the time. Despite such challenges, *Funny Face* was a success with audiences and critics alike. As John Cutts, a reviewer from *Films And Filming* observed at the time:

'*Funny Face* is one of the loveliest musicals ever made. However, what really sets firm the film's total charm is a tender idyll danced by Astaire and Hepburn in a misty flower garden of a riverside church. As they softly whirl through the budding daffodils and gently step on the soft spring grass, the film's charm crystallizes firm and makes solid its gay overwhelming appeal. *Funny Face* is the most original screen musical since *Seven Brides For Seven Brothers* and possibly the most enjoyable since *Singin' In The Rain*.'

STANLEY DONEN (b. 1924) started his dancing career at the young age of sixteen on Broadway, where he met – and was profoundly influenced by – the legendary Gene Kelly. Following Kelly's lead, he headed to Hollywood and continued to forge a career in dance. In 1943 he was assistant choreographer on *Best Foot Forward*. During a stint at MGM, in 1949 he directed his first musical, *On The Town*, starring Kelly, followed by *Singin' In The Rain* in 1952, again with his favourite star Gene Kelly. By this point, he had established himself as one of the foremost musical film directors of his time. He also directed numerous comedies during this period, including *Fearless Fagan* (1952) and *Seven Brides For Seven Brothers* (1954). Donen worked with the all-dancing, all-singing Fred Astaire for the first time in *Royal Wedding* (1951). The partnership was re-established in 1957 in *Funny Face*, but this time Astaire starred alongside Audrey Hepburn. Donen would work with Hepburn again in *Charade* (1963) and *Two For The Road* (1967).

Opposite: Funny Face (1957)
US 41 x 27 in. (104 x 69 cm)
Courtesy of The Reel Poster Gallery

Left: A studio technician, Stanley Donen and photographer Richard Avedon discussing the film's title sequence.

Opposite: Japanese press book cover with black silhouette sleeve.

Above: Funny Face (1957)
US 60 x 40 in. (152 x 102 cm)
(Style B)
Courtesy of The Reel Poster Gallery

Opposite: Funny Face (1957)
US 60 x 40 in. (152 x 102 cm)
(Style A)
Courtesy of The Reel Poster Gallery

Above: Funny Face
(Cenerentola A Parigi) (1957)
Italian 79 x 55 in. (201 x 140 cm)
Art by Ercole Brini
Courtesy of The Reel Poster Gallery

A role made in heaven for Hepburn.
Here we see her enjoying practising her
singing and dancing skills in preparation for
Funny Face. It was necessary for Hepburn
to return to ballet exercises and endless
rehearsals with Eugene Loring, who devised
the film's choreography with Fred Astaire.

Left: American model Dovima (1927–1990)
poses next to a sculpture of a woman in a
scene from the film. *Opposite:* Hepburn
posing for publicity shots for *Funny Face.*

Above: Hepburn practises some of her
snazzy solo dance routines.

Opposite: Funny Face (1957)
US 81 x 81 in. (206 x 206 cm)
Courtesy of The Reel Poster Gallery

RICHARD AVEDON'S (1923–2004) passion for photography began at a young age. When he was ten he snapped the composer Sergei Rachmaninoff, who happened to live above his family home, and this fascination with the famous and iconic would stay with him throughout his life. On setting off to join the Merchant Marines in 1942, his father gave him his first camera as a going-away present, and this allowed him to explore his favourite pastime. When he returned to the United States in 1944, he found work as an advertising photographer for a department store. However, he was soon discovered by Alexey Brodovich, art director of fashion magazine *Harper's Bazaar*. Gaining confidence as a fashion photographer, he set up his own studio in 1946 and began providing photographs for *Vogue* and *Life*. Although his career began as a fashion photographer, Avedon branched out, capturing some of the most momentous events of the twentieth century, from the American civil rights movement in 1963 to the fall of the Berlin Wall in 1989. He was also renowned for his portrait photographs and produced some of the most original and iconic images of his time. His favourite subject was the 1950s model Dovima, who also appeared in *Funny Face* (1957). His most famous photograph of her is entitled *Dovima With Elephants* (1955). In the 1950s he photographed Marilyn Monroe, and in the 60s, the Beatles and Andy Warhol. Challenging classic expectations in portraiture, Richard Avedon is considered perhaps one of the most influential photographers of the twentieth century. His work is currently exhibited in collections at the Museum of Modern Art and the Metropolitan Museum of Art, New York, and in many museums worldwide including the Victoria and Albert Museum, London.

Above: The highest-paid model of her generation, Dovima was Richard Avedon's favourite subject. Here with Hepburn she looks at a *Vogue* magazine on the cover of which she appears. *Opposite: Harper's Bazaar* cover from the same year with photo by Richard Avedon.

Harper's

BAZAAR

October 1956

Incorporating Junior Bazaar

The Jewel Make-Ups—

New Lights, New Lusters

60 cents

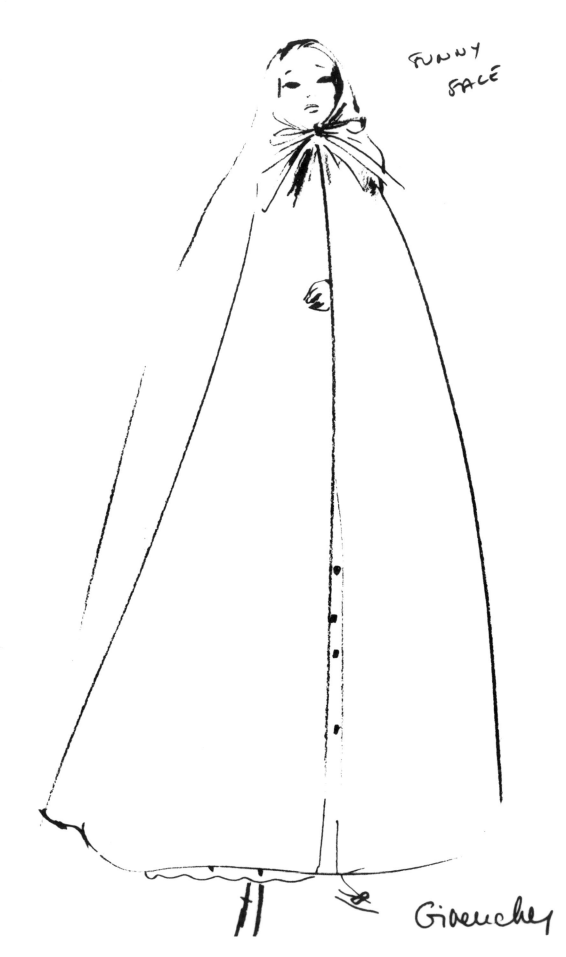

FUNNY FACE

Givenchy

HUBERT DE GIVENCHY (b. 1927) was born in Beauvais, France. While studying at the École des Beaux-Arts in Paris in 1944, he was offered his first part-time job in fashion by Jacques Fath. Having established himself as an up-and-coming couturier working under the direction of a string of famous designers, Givenchy opened the House of Givenchy in 1952. Here he presented his first collection, 'Bettina', after Paris's top model Bettina Graziana. It was a move that brought him huge success and worldwide recognition. Two women represent Givenchy's approach to fashion design in the 50s and 60s: Jackie Kennedy and Audrey Hepburn. He famously dressed the entire Kennedy family for John F. Kennedy's funeral. Givenchy began to dress Hepburn from the beginning of her career and right through until she became a movie star icon. Always immaculately dressed, Hepburn was the perfect model for Givenchy's designs. Such was Hepburn's worldwide fashion impact, that when Givenchy introduced his perfume *L'Interdit* in 1957, he allowed only her to wear it for the first year to create hype around its promotion. In 1968 Givenchy opened his Givenchy Nouvelle Boutique, with a new, exciting prêt-a-porter line more in keeping with the times. In 1988 he sold the House of Givenchy to Moët Hennessy Louis Vuitton (LVMH), but remained head of design until his retirement in 1995.

Left: Original costume sketch by Givenchy of the cape Hepburn wore in *Funny Face*. *Opposite:* Hepburn wears the same sumptuous silk cape for a publicity shot.

FRED ASTAIRE'S character Dick Avery is based on Richard Avedon, known to his friends as Dick Avery. Born Frederic Austerlitz in Nebraska, Fred Astaire (1899–1987) entered show business at the tender age of five, performing a vaudeville act alongside his sister Adele. Their talent took them to Broadway in the 1920s and onto the London stage, where they won great critical acclaim. In 1932, upon Adele's marriage and retirement, Fred headed straight for Hollywood. Although an early Paramount Pictures screen test report on Astaire stated simply, 'Can't sing. Can't act. Slightly balding. Also dances', he has become known as one of the greatest dancers ever to hit the big screen, famed for his pinpoint accuracy and sometimes painstaking perfectionism. He is most renowned for dancing with the legendary Ginger Rogers in a string of films, most notably *Flying Down To Rio* (1933), *The Gay Divorcee* (1934), *Top Hat* (1935), *Swing Time* (1936) and *Shall We Dance* (1937). In 1947 he opened the Fred Astaire Dance Studios in America and Canada. He continued to star in numerous films for both cinema and television until 1981.

Above: Hepburn and Astaire pose for publicity shots for *Funny Face*.
Opposite. For a *Marie Claire*, September 1956 cover story Hepburn wears a striking red dress by Givenchy with matching ballet pumps.

MARIE ★ CLAIRE

NUMÉRO SPÉCIAL DES COLLECTIONS SEPTEMBRE

Toute la nouvelle mode

N° 23 - SEPTEMBRE 1956

PRIX **70** FRS

BELGIQUE 15 FR. SUISSE 1 FR. 30

LE PHOTOGRAPHE DE MODE (FRED ASTAIRE)
ET SON MODÈLE (AUDREY HEPBURN)

Above, opposite and overleaf (pages 86 and 87): Fashion and film meet in Funny Face. Hepburn poses for the 'Take The Picture' sequence.

Above: Hepburn's outfit here started a new fashion: high-necked sweater with tight trousers, white socks and moccasins.

Opposite: Funny Face
(*Das Rosarote Mannequin*) (1957)
German 33 x 23 in. (84 x 58 cm)
(Re-release 1960s)
Courtesy of The Reel Poster Gallery

AUDREY HEPBURN
MOVIE STAR AND FASHION ICON

'If a woman walks into a room and people say, "Oh, what a marvellous dress", then she is badly dressed. If they say, "What a beautiful woman", then she is well dressed.' – Coco Chanel

Audrey Hepburn was one of the most successful and beloved film stars of the twentieth century. Her style has been admired and copied by several generations of young women. Even today, more than a decade after her death, she is still regarded as one of the most beautiful and stylish women in the world. How could Audrey Hepburn have become such a big movie star when she was almost the antithesis of Hollywood's conventional ideal of beauty? And what role did fashion play in the context of her career?

'This girl, single-handed, may make bosoms a thing of the past.' – Billy Wilder

At first, Hepburn's appearance – a skinny, flat-chested, short-haired brunette with bushy eyebrows, elongated neck and size 8 feet – seemed an unlikely recipe for success in Hollywood, where buxom beauties with long – preferably blonde – hair reigned supreme. In the 50s and 60s, Hepburn became the emissary of a new look: an androgynous yet hyper-feminized woman of the world dressed impeccably in modern Parisian chic. Combining disarming innocence and cosmopolitan flair with an unerring sense of style, she emerged in marked contrast to Hollywood's sexually charged notion of what women should be and thus offered a viable alternative for millions of women.

One of the key questions we must ask is how Hepburn – a shy, introverted and delicate person who had little formal training as an actress – could instantly become one of the most popular stars in the history of film. In his book *Who The Hell's In It*, Peter Bogdanovich's vivid account of her transformation in front of the camera provides some clues:

'My first reaction after spending some time with Audrey had been to wonder how anyone of such extraordinary fragility and gentleness, with a profound shyness and self-deprecation, could ... in fact, ever get up in front of a camera and perform? ... An amazingly subtle yet uncanny transformation then happened: this vulnerable, kind and self-effacing woman ... somehow could marshal all of her own sensibilities into a forceful, magical power to express all those qualities, to live and breathe even more naturally than she did in day-to-day life, with all the finest nuances of character and meaning behind her words and looks.' What Hepburn lacked in acting skills she made up for in charisma and screen presence. Her natural beauty, charming spontaneity and graceful posture, coupled with style and elegance, proved to be an irresistible mix.

'Audrey was always more about fashion than movies or acting.' – Stanley Donen

Like no other, Hepburn's star image is inextricably linked to high fashion. From the start, in her first major role as the princess who yearns for a normal life in *Roman Holiday* (1953), Hepburn was highly conscious of her on-screen image. Evincing a distinct flair for style, she

Right: Hepburn wears Givenchy's 'jazzy' grey wool ottoman suit in *Sabrina*.

contributed to costume designer Edith Head's ideas by adding to her look a wide leather belt and a neck scarf, thus making an already pretty outfit even more personal. Hepburn instinctively knew that while Head's designs were very effective, she needed something more. Thanks to her instant stardom – winning an Oscar for her very first performance – she had the freedom to control her look without the usual studio interference.

Hepburn found what she was looking for in the haute couture of Hubert de Givenchy, who had just opened his own fashion house in 1952. His innovative modern designs were ideally suited for her figure and the stylish persona she wanted to create. She began wearing 'Givenchy' in her film and public appearances, publicity articles and fashion magazines, a collaboration and friendship that lasted for over forty years. No other star has ever achieved such a powerful symbiosis with a couturier.

'Thinking of Audrey I remember the extraordinary bond that existed between us. She was capable of enhancing all my creations. And often ideas would come to me when I had her on my mind.' – Hubert de Givenchy

The balance between dress and persona is crucial: a well-designed wardrobe bestows its beauty on the bearer. Givenchy perfectly understood Hepburn's appeal and found the ideal equilibrium between haute couture and her natural beauty and character. Hepburn was never in danger of being overwhelmed by his dresses. Givenchy's fashions not only made Hepburn beautiful – they also helped a shy woman to overcome her insecurities.

'I depend on Givenchy the same way American women depend on their psychiatrists.'
– Audrey Hepburn

Hepburn referred to Givenchy's designs as protective armour: 'Givenchy's creations always gave me a sense of security and confidence, and my work went more easily in the knowledge that I looked absolutely right. I felt the same at my private appearances, Givenchy's outfits gave me "protection" against strange situations and people, because I felt so good

in them. In a certain way one can say that Hubert de Givenchy has "created" me over the years.'

Givenchy's exquisite wardrobe perfectly matched not only Hepburn's figure but her personality as well. While he – as the genius – provided the elegant 'protective armour', she – as his muse – made him famous. Together they forged a new image of femininity: Hepburn's look of a chic cosmopolitan woman; cultured, subtle and with an infectious youthful esprit. Her style caught on immediately, with millions of women admiring and imitating her look.

The Hepburn-Givenchy collaboration created a tremendous synergy that, in the hands of directors Billy Wilder, Stanley Donen and Blake Edwards, found a direct expression in their films. *Sabrina* (1954) and *Funny Face* (1957), both variations on the Cinderella story, depict the transformation of the main character from simple girl to woman of the world. It is no coincidence that Hepburn played these characters so well since the role required a mix of naïveté, charm, sexual/romantic awakening and gamine elegance. In each instance Givenchy's fashion aided the process of transformation.

It was Hepburn who suggested to Billy Wilder the use of Givenchy's designs for *Sabrina*. Wilder quickly realized their importance for the film. Sabrina, a chauffeur's adolescent daughter, falls in love with the son of the wealthy family that employs her father but is ignored by him. She is sent to Paris as a frustrated and unhappy girl and comes back an elegant lady. Emphasizing the transformation, she returns with a completely new wardrobe designed by Givenchy. She tells her father, who plans to pick her up at the train station, that he will hardly recognize her. Impeccably dressed in modern Parisian chic, she looks like she just stepped out of *Vogue*.

'If you should have any difficulties recognizing your daughter, I shall be the most sophisticated woman at the Glencove Station.' – Sabrina

Haute couture plays an important role in the transformation, making Hepburn very special and dramatically increasing her desirability. When Sabrina 'officially' enters the world of the wealthy at the Larabee ball – a key sequence in the movie – she wears a spectacular strapless white ballgown. With her youthful charm, gracious movement and elegant manner, Sabrina and her dress are a total knockout. Literally a showstopper, the dress draws attention to itself, and the narrative progression briefly comes to a halt. By foregrounding the dress, Wilder highlights Sabrina's strategy of using high fashion as an effective means of crossing the dividing class line and finding romantic fulfillment – a beautiful maid in shining armour, 'dressed to kill'. What makes Sabrina so endearing is her seemingly effortless transition (after having had some training by a French baron – a little *Pygmalion* touch); in fact, she is very much at ease in both worlds.

Fashion itself takes centre stage in *Funny Face*. Stanley Donen's ironic look at the fashion world details the transformation of the Greenwich Village bluestocking bookseller Jo Stockton (Audrey Hepburn) into a fashion supermodel while romancing Madison fashion photographer Dick Avery (Fred Astaire). Combining a Cinderella-*Pygmalion* theme with parts of the real-life story of fashion photographer Richard Avedon, the film evolves as a narrativized fashion show, a kind of animated *Vogue*. The lines between fashion show and movie are intentionally blurred and the conventions of fashion photography are cleverly integrated into the fabric of the narrative.

In a first encounter with the 'fashion people' as they invade her quiet bookstore for their photo shoot, Jo declares that fashion is superficial and stupid. But a kiss from Dick Avery and a Givenchy hat accidentally left behind from the shoot trigger her fantasies of romance. Dressed in a combination of loose grey tweed jumper, black sweater and loafers, she puts on the elegant bright yellow hat for her first song-and-dance number – signalling the first step in her transformation. The process is completed in the fashion photography session in Paris. This culminates in the scene in the Louvre when Jo, clearly enjoying her new fashionable self, appears behind a large white marble statue in a magnificent red strapless evening dress, red shoes, white gloves, blue diamond necklace and gamine hairstyle.

Dick Avery – *'Holy Moses! You look fabulous. Stop! Stop!'*
Jo – *'Take the picture!'*

A figure of ethereal beauty – a red silk chiffon stole floating like wings, emulating the *Winged Victory* behind her – she descends the stairs, arms outstretched high. Completely overwhelmed by the vision, her photographer-lover struggles to capture an image of her. Interestingly, the film was not marketed as a romantic high-fashion extravaganza. Instead of depicting Hepburn as a glamorous fashion model, the advertising focused on the 'hip' qualities of its female star – the tagline reading 'Audrey is a hepcat now'. Superimposed on a close-up of her 'funny face', the poster depicts a full-figured Hepburn in an expressive dance pose, wearing her hallmark black turtleneck sweater, trousers, flat shoes and cropped hair. Her arms stretched upward, her face and gestures exude upbeat energy and youthful exuberance.

Breakfast At Tiffany's cemented Hepburn's dual status as movie star and fashion icon. Commonly regarded as Hepburn's signature piece, the film and its poster have subsequently gained cult status. More upbeat than the Truman Capote novella it is based on, Blake Edwards's movie version focuses on a Manhattan call-girl (Hepburn) who becomes romantically involved with an aspiring writer, Paul (George Peppard), who himself is 'patronized' by a wealthy woman. Unlike the novel, the film – in typical Hollywood manner – offers a happy ending through the redemptive power of true love.

Hepburn plays the attractive but highly dysfunctional Holly Golightly who somehow manages to eke out a living through prostitution and yet remain completely innocent at heart.

In a career spanning over forty years, **ROBERT MCGINNIS** (b. 1926) has distinguished himself as a painter of beautiful women and Western landscapes. As a young man, the Cincinnati-born artist studied fine art at Ohio State University by day and commercial art at the Central Academy of Commercial Art by night. He began his career as an animation apprentice at Disney Studios before moving on to design film and advertising posters. He is responsible for no fewer than seven James Bond marketing campaigns, including *Thunderball* (1965) and *You Only Live Twice* (1967) as well as over forty other film posters for classics such as *Breakfast At Tiffany's* (1961), *Barbarella* (1968) and *The Odd Couple* (1968).

Opposite: Breakfast At Tiffany's (1961)
US 41 x 27 in. (104 x 69 cm)
Art by Robert E. McGinnis
Courtesy of The Reel Poster Gallery

This seemingly independent, carefree and high-spirited woman shows a vulnerability that makes her endearing to the audience. The sentimental song 'Moon River' evokes her rural roots and a sense of innocence and longing. Her complex character is best summarized in the words of one of her friends, producer O. J. Berman (Martin Balsam): 'She's a *real* phony.'

The opening sequence of *Breakfast At Tiffany's* sets the tone for the movie. A beautiful woman dressed in a stunning evening gown emerges from a yellow cab in the early morning hours to look at Tiffany's display windows. Gazing at the luxury items behind the glass, she sips coffee from a paper cup and nibbles at a Danish. Holly later explains to Paul that she goes to Tiffany's when she suffers one of her periodic panic attacks, which she calls 'the mean reds'.

'When I get [the mean reds] the only thing that does any good is to jump into a cab and go to Tiffany's. Calms me down right away. If I could find a real place to make me feel like Tiffany's, then I'd buy some furniture and give the cat a name.' – Holly Golightly

The 150-year-old store, described as 'the marriage of wealth and decorative arts', and Givenchy's haute couture are powerful antidotes to the 'mean reds'. Conjuring up associations of wealth, luxury, prestige and refinement, they give Holly a feeling of security, identity and social standing that she has been striving for her whole life. The paper cup and Danish pastry in Holly's hand are a decided contrast to an otherwise perfect match of high chic and luxurious Tiffany's. Seeing her munching on a Danish provides a point of identification, making an otherwise ultra-stylish model more accessible for the audience.

Like the film, the poster itself has become a classic, commanding high prices at galleries and auctions. Referring to the opening sequence, it depicts the ultra-slim figure of Hepburn wearing a gorgeous black evening gown and carrying an elongated cigarette holder. Highlighting her elegance and stylishness, the poster presents Hepburn as a hyper-feminine woman – the embodiment of an idealized feminine identity. The cat on her shoulder gives an otherwise elusive fashion model – someone who might come across as too stylish, too perfect, too beautiful – more grounding. Sipping coffee from a paper cup or having a cat on the shoulder are perfect examples of how Hepburn's quirky persona managed to combine high fashion with the simple things in life, bringing high fashion out of the stratosphere and into the realms of possibility for young, middle-class female viewers. According to *Variety*, stars are generally 'not expected to look like designers' models but like individuals reflecting their own personalities while satisfying the screen image expectations of fans.' Audrey Hepburn was very special: in her case star image and fashion were synonymous. The collaboration with Givenchy generated a powerful synergy that extended far beyond her movies. Hepburn has not lost anything of her immense popularity and appeal, as magazine polls show. In her dual role as movie star and fashion icon, Audrey Hepburn will be with us for a long time to come.

Opposite: The black dress, in long or short versions, became a fashion symbol of the period.

ANDREAS TIMMER

BREAKFAST AT TIFFANY'S (1961)

Starring

Holly Golightly	**AUDREY HEPBURN**
Paul 'Fred' Varjak	**GEORGE PEPPARD**
2-E (Mrs Failenson)	**PATRICIA NEAL**
Doc Golightly	**BUDDY EBSEN**
O. J. Berman	**MARTIN BALSAM**
Cat (as Cat)	**ORANGEY**
Mr Yunioshi	**MICKEY ROONEY**

Directed by	**BLAKE EDWARDS**
Original Screenplay by	**GEORGE AXELROD** **(BASED ON A NOVEL BY TRUMAN CAPOTE)**
Cinematography by	**FRANZ PLANER AND PHILIP H. LATHROP**
Costume Design by	**HUBERT DE GIVENCHY (AUDREY HEPBURN) AND PAULINE TRIGERE (PATRICIA NEAL)**
Original Music by	**HENRY MANCINI**

ACADEMY AWARD NOMINATIONS

AUDREY HEPBURN
Best Actress in a Leading Role

ROLAND ANDERSON, HAL PEREIRA, SAM COMER AND RAY MOYER
Best Art Direction / Set Decoration

GEORGE AXELROD
Best Writing / Screenplay Based on Material from Another Medium

ACADEMY AWARDS WON

HENRY MANCINI AND JOHNNY MERCER
Best Music (Original Song)

HENRY MANCINI
Best Music Score / Dramatic or Comedy Picture

BREAKFAST AT TIFFANY'S

More than any other, *Breakfast At Tiffany's* is perhaps *the* quintessential Hepburn movie. Her image as Holly Golightly has achieved iconic status and the film represents the pinnacle of her acting career. Hepburn plays the part of a young and extraordinarily unconventional but sophisticated lady living the high life in New York with her cat. Using her formally trained airs and graces she works as a high-priced call-girl. Despite being perhaps an unlikely choice to play the protagonist from Truman Capote's 1958 original novella, Hepburn's 'innocent' interpretation is perhaps the very reason the character became so endearing.

George Peppard plays the part of Paul 'Fred' Varjak, a struggling writer who moves into Holly's apartment block. Varjak's expenses are provided for by his 'sugar-mummy', Mrs Failenson (Patricia Neal). An innocent friendship develops between Holly and Paul. Holly has her heart set on marrying into money and flitters from man to man, whilst Paul tries to shield her from the heartbreaks that inevitably come her way. Paul is charmed by her natural beauty and free spirit but Holly's determination obscures her from seeing the connection between them.

An unexpected visit by Holly's ex-husband, Doc Golightly (played by Buddy Ebsen) gives an insight into Holly's past and brings Holly and Paul closer. In contrast to Capote's original dark ending where Holly Golightly decides to go off travelling alone after a number of failed affairs, the film's plot offers a more romantic conclusion whereby Paul and Holly finally get together. It was a decision that upset Capote, who felt it undermined the outlook of a book about a hedonist who enjoys a spontaneous life of non-conformity.

The film was adapted for the screen by George Axelrod, who was also responsible for writing many other Hollywood classics, including *The Seven Year Itch* (1955), *Bus Stop* (1956) and *The Manchurian Candidate* (1962). Axelrod had worked on the screenplay of *Breakfast At Tiffany's* with John Frankenheimer, who was originally to have been the film's director. (The two did subsequently work together as director/screenwriter on *The Manchurian Candidate*.) The co-starring role of Paul Varjak was originally offered to Steve McQueen. But because he was still under contract for the hit television serial *Wanted: Dead Or Alive*, McQueen was unable to accept.

An immediate hit, *Breakfast At Tiffany's* box-office receipts more than recouped its budget of around $2 million. Hepburn's salary was $750,000 – a far cry from the $15,000 she had received for making *Sabrina* only seven years earlier.

In a review for the *New York Times* upon the film's release, A.H. Weiler wrote:

'*A completely unbelievable but wholly captivating flight into fantasy. Above all, it has the over-powering attribute known as Audrey Hepburn, who, despite her normal, startled-faun exterior, now is displaying a fey, comic talent that should enchant Truman Capote, who created the amoral pixie she portrays, as well as moviegoers meeting her for the first time. All the quick-silverish explanations still have the character as implausible as ever. But in the person of Miss Hepburn, she is a genuinely charming, elfin waif who will be believed and adored.*'

The grandson of silent-screen director J. Gordon Edwards, **BLAKE EDWARDS** (b. 1922) was born in Tulsa, Oklahoma. His career began in 1943 with small acting parts before he started writing scripts for the screen and radio. His first directing opportunity came in 1955 with the musical film *Bring Your Smile Along*. This was followed by a number of successful movies for Universal Studios. Three of his most renowned films, *Breakfast At Tiffany's* (1961), *Days Of Wine And Roses* (1962) and *The Pink Panther* (1963) preceded a successful string of Pink Panther films starring Peter Sellers. He also produced other classics such as *The Great Race* (1965), *The Party* (1968) and *10* (1979). In 1983 he was nominated for an Oscar for Best Screenplay for *Victor/Victoria* in which he directed his wife Julie Andrews. He received an Honorary Academy Award in 2004 in recognition of his contribution to the big screen.

Opposite: Breakfast At Tiffany's (1961)
US 41 x 27 in. (104 x 69 cm)
(Special)
Art by Robert E. McGinnis
Courtesy of Tarek AbuZayyed

Born in Michigan, **GEORGE PEPPARD**
(1928–1994) studied acting at Carnegie
Tech in Pittsburgh and then at The Actor's
Studio. It wasn't long before he stood out
as a promising young star and with the
help of his charming good looks he was
quickly hired to act on Broadway and
television. His film career was launched as
Cadet Robert Marquales in *The Strange
One* (1957), a role he had previously
played on Broadway. Sadly, he was often
cast in undemanding roles that did not
allow his true ability to shine. Peppard is
most renowned for his role as Hepburn's
love interest in *Breakfast At Tiffany's*
(1961). The on-screen chemistry between
them was enchanting and he proved
himself to be the perfect man for the role.

Above and right: Where Ivy League meets
haute couture: Hepburn and Peppard pose
for publicity shots.

Above: Breakfast At Tiffany's
(Colazione Da Tiffany) (1961)
Italian 79 x 55 in. (201 x 140 cm)
(Style B)
Art by Ercole Brini
Courtesy of The Reel Poster Gallery

Opposite: Breakfast At Tiffany's
(Colazione Da Tiffany) (1961)
Italian 79 x 55 in. (201 x 140 cm)
(Style A)
Art by Ercole Brini
Courtesy of Tarek AbuZayyed

E. BRINI
AUDREY HEPBURN
COLAZIONE
DA
TIFFANY
UNA PRODUZIONE JUROW-SHEPHERD
CON GEORGE PEPPARD
E CON PATRICIA NEAL
BUDDY EBSEN
MARTIN BALSAM
VILALLONGA
E MICKEY ROONEY
TECHNICOLOR
Paramount Films
DIRETTO DA BLAKE EDWARDS • SCENEGGIATURA DI GEORGE AXELROD
PRODOTTO DA MARTIN JUROW E RICHARD SHEPHERD
TRATTO DA UN ROMANZO DI TRUMAN CAPOTE MUSICA DI HENRY MANCINI
RIPALTA Industrie Grafiche - Milano - 1961
AVVERTENZA

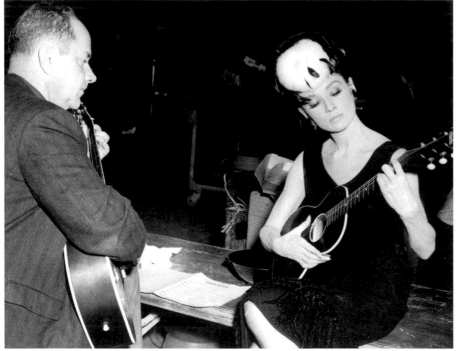

Born in Cleveland, Ohio, **HENRY MANCINI** (1924–1994) went on to become one of the greatest television and film composers of his time. Following the war he spent a few years struggling as a freelance arranger and musician. In 1952 Mancini's music was used in an Abott and Costello film, *Lost In Alaska*. He then became the house arranger for over 100 Universal-International films, including most notably *The Glenn Miller Story* in 1953 and *The Benny Goodman Story* in 1955. But Mancini's personal favourite was the score he wrote for *Touch Of Evil* in 1958, which was the piece that finally launched his career. Mancini worked with director Blake Edwards on over thirty films and television programmes during the course of his career. It was a fruitful collaboration resulting in, among others, *Peter Gunn*, a television series that ran from 1958 until 1961, the *Pink Panther* films and *The Party* (1968). In 1961 he wrote the enchanting 'Moon River' with lyricist Johnny Mercer, which has since been re-recorded countless times. Yet Mancini always believed Hepburn's version in *Breakfast At Tiffany's* to be the definitive one. He thought it sounded like it had been written exclusively for her. Mancini also wrote the music for Hepburn's later films, *Charade* (1963), *Two For The Road* (1967) and *Wait Until Dark* (1967). During his outstanding career, his music was used in over 500 films, although he was not credited for most of them. He received numerous Oscar nominations and won four – two for Best Song and Best Score for *Breakfast At Tiffany's* (1961) and one each for the scores of *Days Of Wine And Roses* (1962), and *Victor/Victoria* (1982). Mancini's timeless music continues to be used today.

Above: Henry Mancini holds his Oscar backstage at the Academy Awards with Cyd Charisse and Tony Martin (9 April 1962). *Below:* Hepburn and her guitar instructor practise 'Moon River' on the set of *Breakfast At Tiffany's*. *Opposite:* Popular Italian soundtrack singer/composer Nico Fidenco sung his version of 'Moon River' in Italian which was renamed 'Colazione Da Tiffany's'.

Opposite: Breakfast At Tiffany's (Colazione Da Tiffany) (1961) Italian 28 x 13 in. (71 x 33 cm) Movie soundtrack tie-in poster

NICO FIDENCO

CANTA

COLAZIONE DA TIFFANY'S

E

AUDREY

**DAL FILM PARAMOUNT
COLAZIONE DA TIFFANY'S**

E' UN DISCO

Known as **MCP, RAMÓN MARTÍ, JOSEP CLAVÉ** and **HERNÁN PICÓ** formed a graphic design company in Barcelona that produced artwork for commercial advertising campaigns. Established in the 30s and continuing to function until 1970, the company specialized in designing posters for the film industry. Between 1945 and 1965, MCP's workload was immense and they employed over twenty designers, one of whom was the prominent Spanish illustrator Macario Gómez. With a vast catalogue of film poster designs to their name, MCP were responsible for the Spanish posters for *The Asphalt Jungle* (1950), *The Bad And The Beautiful* (1953) and *The Big Heat* (1953) as well as *Breakfast At Tiffany's* (1961).

Left: Hepburn begins filming *Breakfast At Tiffany's* in New York wearing the famed Tiffany Diamond necklace valued at $544,500. The opening scene of the film marked the first time that motion-picture cameras had been allowed inside Tiffany's. The Tiffany Diamond weighed 128.51 carats and remained in the store.

Opposite: Breakfast At Tiffany's (Desayuno Con Diamantes) (1961)
Spanish 39 x 28 in. (99 x 71 cm)
Art by Martí, Clavé & Picó (MCP)
Courtesy of The Reel Poster Gallery

During filming, Paramount took advantage
of the opportunity to take publicity shots of
Hepburn inside Tiffany's. Many of these
were subsequently used in various
international advertising campaigns.

Above and left: While Hepburn and Peppard succeed in controlling fits of laughter, leading to a rain-soaked kiss during the filming of *Breakfast At Tiffany's*, 'Cat' contemplates his escape to a warmer, drier place.

Above: Breakfast At Tiffany's
(Colazione Da Tiffany) (1961)
Italian 27 x 19 in. (69 x 48 cm)
two different styles.
Courtesy of The Reel Poster Gallery

Opposite: Breakfast At Tiffany's
(Colazione Da Tiffany) (1961)
Italian 19 x 27 in. (48 x 69 cm)
Courtesy of The Reel Poster Gallery

Hepburn and George Peppard wearing their 'stolen' party masks from 'The Things We've Never Done' scene.

Left: Breakfast At Tiffany's (1961)
Japanese 60 x 20 in. (152 x 51 cm)
(Re-release 1969)
Courtesy of Amit & Vanisha Bhatia

Opposite: Breakfast At Tiffany's (1961)
Japanese 12 x 8 in. (30 x 20 cm)
Press book cover

ティファニーで朝食を

JOSEF VYLET'AL (b. 1940) was born in Brno, Czechoslovakia. He created his first poster in 1963, during a burst of creativity in Czech film-poster art. By the end of the 70s he had exceeded over a hundred film poster commissions and also worked as a theatre and film art director. As a painter and graphic designer, he typically interweaves collage with painting and a light network of drawings that produce a surrealistic sense of psychological tension. This effect is never clearer than in his striking poster design for *Breakfast At Tiffany's* (1961).

Left: Hepburn poses behind a quirky prop from her apartment in *Breakfast At Tiffany's.*

Opposite: Breakfast At Tiffany's
(*Snídaně U Tiffany Ho*) (1961)
Czechoslovakian 33 x 23 in. (84 x 58 cm)
Art by Josef Vylet'al

přepis stejnojmenné knihy Trumana Capota
v hlavní úloze AUDREY HEPBURNOVÁ
režie: Blake Edwards ✶✶✶✶ film USA

Reminiscent of Albert Hirschfeld's
caricature style, illustrator **CRISTIANO**
perfectly captures the zany slapstick tone
of the party scene – a scene that was
totally improvised by director Blake
Edwards. This memorable scene allowed
Edwards to make his distinctive mark on
the movie – a prelude to his 1968 film
The Party starring Peter Sellers.

Opposite: Breakfast At Tiffany's (1961)
Swedish 6 x 5 in. (15 x 13 cm)
Promotional booklet (back cover)
Art by D. Cristiano

Above: Life goes on in the city as Hepburn
prepares for the opening scene at Tiffany's.

Above: Posing for publicity shots, Hepburn wears a black cocktail dress in silk cloqué by Givenchy from his Autumn/Winter 1960/1 collection. *Opposite:* Wearing the same dress on the cover of French *Elle* magazine (January 5th 1962).

ELLE

N° 837

N.F. - SUISSE : 1 FR. S. - GRANDE-BRETAGNE : 1 9 d - CANADA 25 CENTS - ITALIE 140 LIRES - 5 JANVIER 1962

Deux
ans après:
L'ensorcelante
Audrey Hepburn
revient

Modèles
bien chauds
pour
froids week-ends

Pour vous
et votre maison
le Blanc
62

AUDREY STYLE
HER ENDURING MAGIC LIVES ON

More than beauty, more than charm, more than sex appeal, her style is subtle, mysterious – and irresistible. The allure of Audrey Hepburn is as potent today as it ever was at the height of her career. Her image continues to sell millions of luxury goods and glossy magazines and to inspire contemporary fashion designers.

Ironically, it was a passion for fashion that led, if somewhat indirectly, to Audrey Hepburn's impact on Hollywood. The promise of wearing and keeping a Dior couture costume, a month in the South of France in the middle of a bitterly cold British winter plus a generous fee, was too much for any girl to resist. With this in mind, Hepburn accepted a part in a trivial farce called *Monte Carlo Baby* (1952). As it turned out, being in the right place at the right time paid off. A chance meeting with the French novelist Colette in Monte Carlo led to the leading role in *Gigi* on Broadway. And before she ever had the chance to set foot on stage, Hepburn was screen-tested by William Wyler for the role of the young Princess Ann in *Roman Holiday* (1953). The rest, as they say, is history.

It was not that she invented new fashions or even that she was conventionally beautiful. Nevertheless, she made a ballgown, a little black dress, or pair of Capris look effortlessly chic. As Dominick Dunne once said: 'The word *elegant* was invented for her.' This natural elegance could have something to do with Hepburn having worked as a fashion model and dancer, already having learnt how to project her best aspects to the camera. What she wore therefore became an important part of her craft, giving her the boost of confidence she needed to become the women she portrayed on-screen. As she admitted at the time: 'Some people dream of having a big swimming pool – with me, it's closets.'

When Hepburn appeared in *Roman Holiday*, Dior's New Look silhouette of fitted bodice and big skirt dominated fashion. Meanwhile, in the US, designer Claire McCardell believed women's clothes should be versatile, comfortable, flattering and easy to care for.

'I never think of myself as an icon. What is in other people's minds is not in my mind. I just do my thing.'
Audrey Hepburn

Opposite: Hepburn looking très chic in a little black dress, while her dog, Famous, looks on. Photographed by Bob Willoughby on the set of *Paris When It Sizzles* (1962) for French *Vogue*.

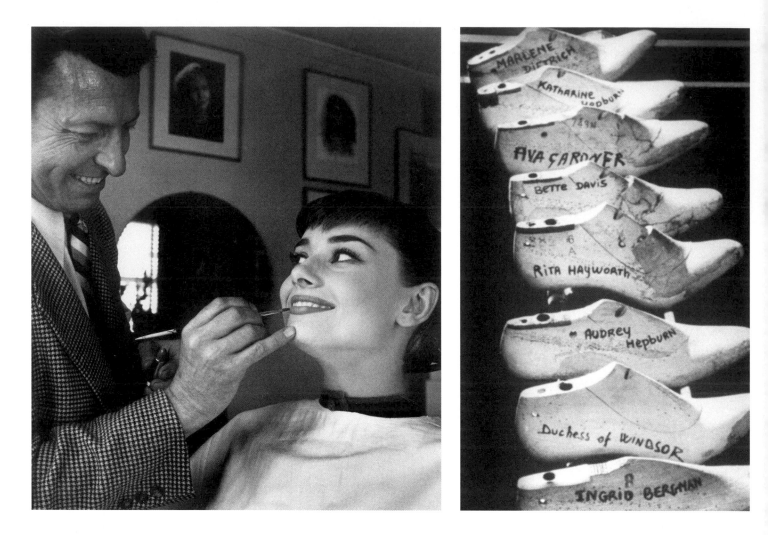

Edith Head, who designed the costumes for the movie, was obviously influenced by both aesthetics. The costume changes included a ballgown and a formal suit with hat, gloves and bag. But it was the popular circle skirt and classic white blouse Hepburn wore throughout the greater part of the movie that she made her own. This occurred by simply rolling up the sleeves of the shirt, and adding a jaunty neckerchief and a wide belt to flatter her minute twenty-inch waist. In doing so, she astutely portrayed the feeling of a more relaxed way to dress – the girl next door. For although in retrospect the 50s seem to have been a formally dressed period, when women clad themselves in gloves, hat, bag, stole and shoes just so, they were actually a time of increasing casualness.

Fifties styling, without the constrictions of corset and non-stretch fabrics, continues to fascinate contemporary designers. Miuccia Prada is particularly fond of the period, as is Roland Mouret, whose hourglass-shape cocktail dress became every modern starlet's must-have in 2005.

During her long career, Audrey made no bones about relying on hair and make-up professionals to present her in the best light. Alberto and Grazia Rossi, the celebrated husband- and-wife team at Paramount, were assigned to work with Hepburn on *Roman Holiday* where she really sparkled. Rossi was responsible for creating the now legendary 'Audrey Hepburn eyes' – her most alluring facial feature. To emphasize the freshness and clarity of her almond-shaped eyes, he adopted a slow process of applying mascara and then separating each eyelash. Eyeliner was applied to the top lid only. Her eyebrows were kept full and gently shaped upwards. Her strong jawline was cleverly balanced by highlighting

Above left: Wally Westbrook, one of the famous dynasty of Hollywood make-up men preparing Hepburn for publicity shots for Paramount Pictures, 1953. *Above:* Wooden shoe lasts of celebrated women at shoemaker Salvatore Ferragamo. *Opposite:* Couturier Hubert de Givenchy adjusts the toile for the costume she wears to open the fashion-show sequence in *Funny Face.*

the temples. The Rossis continued to work with Hepburn throughout her career, adapting her make-up to suit the role. Wally Westbrook was another industry professional who regularly worked on Audrey's make-up.

Another of Audrey's lucky finds and life-long collaborators was the celebrated Italian shoemaker Salvatore Ferragamo. They met in Rome, where there was plenty of time for shopping jaunts during the production of *Roman Holiday*. This was a leisurely six-month shoot, so it was not surprising Audrey found her way to Ferragamo. Salvatore Ferragamo counted most of the best-dressed women of the mid twentieth century as his clients, including Sophia Loren, Greta Garbo, Lauren Bacall and the Duchess of Windsor. He was delighted to make shoes for Audrey who had long, slender, size 8 feet perfectly in proportion with her height. She remained a loyal client for the rest of her life, wearing his heels as a young woman and his driving moccasins in her favourite blue and white into her sixties.

When Audrey appeared in *Sabrina* (1954) a dramatic transformation had taken place in her appearance. The comeback of haute couture resulted in fashion novelty, luxury and quality – and above all, a feeling of Frenchness. For Audrey it was the start of a beautiful friendship and lifelong collaboration with the Paris couturier, Hubert de Givenchy. He created a sensation with his debut collection of *separables*, or separates, which could

Above left: About to begin filming *Breakfast At Tiffany's* (1961), Hepburn looks exquisite in black Givenchy dress and one of the store's most expensive diamond necklaces. *Above:* Chanel's Karl Lagerfeld wittily updates the 'Audrey Look' for the Autumn/Winter 2005 collection. *Opposite left:* Hepburn's affection for dancer's kit – capri trousers, black jumper and flat pumps – looks as hip now as it did when she posed for this promotional portrait for Billy Wilder's film *Sabrina*. *Opposite right:* New design talent at Givenchy, Ricardo Tisci, redefines a capri trouser ensemble in shapely form for Spring/Summer 2006.

be mixed and matched at will. Most famous was his Bettina blouse made of simple cotton shirting, so named after one of his models and press attaché. On the strength of this early success, Givenchy was fêted internationally and was soon to find his muse.

Before Givenchy set up on his own he worked for Jacques Fath, who was the first French designer to acknowledge a more youthful market for his sophisticated tailored designs. Then he assisted the serious Robert Piquet. A year later he moved to Lucien Lelong whose firm, Christian Dior, Pierre Balmain had just left; and finally to the flamboyant Elsa Schiaparelli. Yet it was Cristóbal Balenciaga, the great Spanish designer, who Givenchy most admired and although they never worked together, they were close friends and mutually supportive.

The costumes Audrey chose for *Sabrina* from Givenchy's collection – just three perfect ensembles: a white organza ballgown embroidered in black, decorated with jet beads (number 808 of the 1953 spring/summer collection, called 'Inez de Castro'); a jazzy Oxford-grey fitted grey suit; and a black satin cocktail dress which he called 'décolleté Sabrina' and cost $560 – were each accessorized with chic little hats. All would easily pass today as models straight off the catwalk.

Nowadays, the house of Givenchy is a bit like Stradivarius. It has been passed from owner to owner, designer to designer, to John Galliano, Alexander McQueen, Julian Macdonald

and now to Ricardo Tisci. Tisci seems to be the designer who has at last realized the spirit of Givenchy but has injected equal measures of his own clever ideas to the brand.

Hubert de Givenchy, meanwhile, gives us an idea of the thinking behind Hepburn's style in his behind-the-scenes comments during the filming of *Sabrina*. He said of Hepburn: 'She knew exactly how to shape her strong, independent image. This naturally extended to the way she dressed. And she always took the clothes created for her one step further by adding something of her own, some small personal detail which enhanced the whole. But it was not only elegance that she enhanced. She heightened the impact of the entire design.' Audrey loved Givenchy's clothes because 'they are clothes without ornament, with everything stripped away. You can wear Hubert's clothes until they are worn out and still look elegant.'

From then on Givenchy was Audrey's official costume designer and she his muse. Together they continued on a creative curve in film after film: *Funny Face* (1957); *Breakfast At Tiffany's* (1961); *Paris When It Sizzles* (1964) and finally Sidney Sheldon's *Bloodline* (1979).

Audrey sang and danced through *Funny Face*, the ultimate fashion musical, in wonderfully sophisticated Givenchy costumes. That movie made more people aspire to become designers than perhaps any other film. So many of the looks have carried forward: her affection for wearing all black, now every woman's standard; and she really knew how to wear the trench — with the right amount of buttons closed and nonchalantly belted. The trench coat continues to be the one item at the top of every fashionista's must-have list. Coco Chanel may have been the first couturier to invent the little black dress, but it

Above left: Hepburn wears Givenchy's beautifully tailored red coat on the set of *Breakfast At Tiffany's*. *Above:* Duplicating the eye-catching collar and bold statement buttons, this white wool coat squares up for summer 2006 by Pucci. *Opposite left:* Fresh white, the modernist's version of the classic trench coat designed for Summer 2006 by the French label, Celine. *Opposite right:* Wearing a headscarf and trench coat in the 60s. Hepburn's natural style transformed the plainest clothes into the height of elegance.

was Audrey Hepburn who immortalized the LBD in *Breakfast At Tiffany's*. This, along with upswept hairstyles, multiple strings of pearls, over-sized sunglasses, wearing a man's shirt and little else, carrying a chain-handled bag, tightly wrapping a trench coat instead of buttoning it . . . In fact, there is a fashion styling idea in practically every frame.

Karl Lagerfeld for Chanel, albeit with tongue in cheek, knows the power of Audrey's iconic image and Jean Paul Gaultier works his modern magic on the LBD for Hermès. Moreover, in the UK the designers at Jean Muir consistently play their hand in creating chic new angles on this timeless classic.

Repeatedly, what Hepburn wore in the movies has bounced back into fashion with new vigour. She could not get enough of Givenchy's coats, usually with boat or funnel necklines with soft shoulders and large, decorative buttons. They became a private indulgence and she chose to wear them at every opportunity in her movies. In *Paris When It Sizzles* (1964), set on location in Paris in spring, the stand-out costumes were Givenchy's fresh, neat pastel-coloured suits and dresses, often trimmed at the waist with a bow. All with matching hats, shoes and bag. All back in fashion decades later. Fresh and smart in white at Pucci. Big and bold at Burberry. And always appropriate from the designers at Jean Muir. Balenciaga once said: 'The secret of elegance is elimination,' and Hepburn believed that. For those who love fashion, you can be sure there will always be a little piece of Audrey in the wardrobe to remind us of her delightfully understated and immensely chic presence.

JUNE MARSH

PARIS WHEN IT SIZZLES (1964)

Starring

Richard Benson	**WILLIAM HOLDEN**
Gabrielle Simpson	**AUDREY HEPBURN**
Alexander Meyerheim	**NOEL COWARD**
Maurice/Philippe	**TONY CURTIS**
Cameo appearance (Uncredited)	**MARLENE DIETRICH**
Mr Hyde Cameo appearance (Uncredited)	**MEL FERRER**

Directed by	**RICHARD QUINE**
Original Screenplay by	**GEORGE AXELROD (BASED ON A NOVEL BY JULIEN DUVIVIER AND HENRI JEANSON)**
Cinematography by	**CHARLES LANG AND CLAUDE RENOIR (UNCREDITED)**
Costume Design by	**HUBERT DE GIVENCHY**

PARIS WHEN IT SIZZLES

Audrey Hepburn and William Holden were reunited in *Paris When It Sizzles* ten years after they first appeared together in *Sabrina*. Holden plays the part of a well-known but lackadaisical writer, Rick Benson, who has been in Paris supposedly working on a script for months. When he receives a two-day deadline from his producer, he quickly hires a live-in secretary, Gabrielle Simpson (Hepburn) to help him finish writing *The Girl Who Stole The Eiffel Tower*. Rick is in desperate need of inspiration and when Gabrielle mentions that she has a date planned for Bastille Day, 14th July, he thinks he has found it . . . He begins to dictate a simple 'boy meets girl' story, but then interweaves an array of gangsters, inspectors and fancy-dress parties into the mix – all of which they enact in a series of fantastical vignettes. As Rick and Gabrielle spend time contemplating the fate of the lovers in the story, they fall in love.

With Hollywood craftsmanship and using rich Technicolor, director Richard Quine created this stylized light-hearted spoof on various cinematic genres. He exploited the playful champagne-induced chemistry between Hepburn and Holden, which injected an impelling energy into the rather sketchy dialogue and plot. Among others, Quine also directed *Bell Book And Candle* (1958), *The World Of Suzie Wong* (1960) and *Hotel* (1967). With Christian Dior and Givenchy costume design and cameo appearances by Tony Curtis, Noel Coward, Mel Ferrer, Robert Wagner and Marlene Dietrich, *Paris When It Sizzles* is interspersed with film industry gags, its manic energy offering a light-hearted exposé of elegant 60s chic. The package even included Givenchy's famous perfume, for which he received screen credit.

Although filmed in 1962, *Paris When It Sizzles* was not released until 1964. The film's opening scene begins near Monaco and moves to the suburbs of Paris, ending at the Eiffel Tower. Thanks to cinematographers Charles Lang and Claude Renoir, *Paris When It Sizzles* has stunning visual appeal. Although in its day the film was not well received by many influential film critics, the performances of its two leads remain endearing.

Hepburn had previously worked with Charles Lang on *Sabrina* and *Charade*. This was also her second collaboration with Fred Astaire, who sings a tune. The film was a slightly more whimsical comedy than Hepburn fans were accustomed to, but the interplay with William Holden offers a finale whereby he finally gets the girl he had missed out on ten years earlier in *Sabrina*.

Born in Detroit, Michigan, **RICHARD QUINE** (1920–1989) entered show business at the age of eleven on Broadway. At fourteen he appeared in John Ford's *The World Moves On* (1934) and he went on to act on stage, radio and film. In 1948 Quine gave up his acting career to direct and produce movies. His skills were demonstrated in the thriller *Pushover* (1954), the musical *My Sister Eileen* (1955) and the comedy *The Solid Gold Cadillac* (1956). It was the genre of light comedy that most appealed to Quine. But as audience expectations began to change in the 60s and 70s, the director's appeal waned. His final film was *The Prisoner Of Zenda* (1979), starring Peter Sellers.

Opposite: Paris When It Sizzles (1964)
US 41 x 27 in. (104 x 69 cm)

WILLIAM HOLDEN (1918–1981) played his first starring role as a boxer/violinist opposite Barbara Stanwyck in *Golden Boy* (1939). On his return from the war he played two challenging roles that turned him into an international star: as Joe Gillis in *Sunset Boulevard* (1950), for which he received his first Academy Award nomination, and as Paul Verrall in *Born Yesterday* (1950). In 1953 he played the part of a sergeant suspected of being a Nazi spy in Billy Wilder's *Stalag 17*. Marking the peak of his career, Holden's performance led to his only Academy Award. He went on to star in classics such as *The Bridge Over The River Kwai* (1957), *The Wild Bunch* (1969) and *Network* (1976).

Opposite: Paris When It Sizzles
(*Paris – Tu – Y Yo*) (1964)
Spanish 39 x 27 in. (99 x 69 cm)
(Printed in Italy)
Art by Ercole Brini
Courtesy of The Reel Poster Gallery

Opposite: Paris When It Sizzles
(Zusammen In Paris) (1964)
German 33 x 23 in. (84 x 58 cm)
Art by Rolf Goetze
Courtesy of The Reel Poster Gallery

あなたと私が一緒になる…その日…パリ祭！ エッフェル塔もツイストす

《総天然色》

パリで一緒に

でシャレたヘプバーンの最新作!!

ウィリアム・ホールデン
オードリー・ヘプバーン

リチャード・クワイン監督
リチャード・クワイン
ジョージ・アクセルロッド 〉製作
主題歌 リプリーズ・レコード

Paris WHEN IT SIZZLES

パラマウント映画

Paris When It Sizzles (1964)
Japanese 28 x 40 in. (71 x 102 cm)
Courtesy of The Reel Poster Gallery

As usual, Hepburn is very lovely to look at in *Paris When It Sizzles*, dressed in Givenchy.

Left: Having fun dressed in medieval style costume, Hepburn wears a gown made from cream silk brocade edged with black velvet. *Opposite:* Her femininity shines through clad in a leather flight suit. Costumes by Givenchy. Photos by Bob Willoughby.

BOB WILLOUGHBY (b. 1927) was born in Los Angeles. His career began as an assistant photographer, but his break came when he was commissioned by *Harper's Bazaar* to provide photographs for articles on arts and culture. He was employed as a 'special' photographer on films such as *Limelight* (1952), *Hans Christian Andersen* (1952), *The Desert Rats* (1953) and *A Star Is Born* (1954). One of his photographs for the latter was used as his first cover for *Life* magazine. He was also responsible for the publicity photographs of some of the most successful films of the 50s, 60s and 70s, including *The Man With The Golden Arm* (1955), *My Fair Lady* (1964), *The Graduate* (1967), *Rosemary's Baby* (1968) and *Klute* (1971). As a 'special' photographer with a skilful feel for the personality of his subjects, Willoughby was able to enter the lives of Hollywood stars, directors and personalities and provide a perceptive insight into what went on behind the scenes and on the sets. In 1953 Willoughby met Hepburn for the first time to photograph her for the publicity of *Roman Holiday*. He said of her: 'She was one of the most beautiful women I have ever photographed, and yet, I felt all her beauty came from inside, and it radiated out to everyone around her.' Further to his outstanding influence as a photographer, Willoughby conceived and actualized new photographic techniques and equipment. He created the first remote-controlled camera for use on-set. His work continues to be shown worldwide and is in permanent collections at the National Portrait Gallery, Washington, DC; the National Portrait Gallery, London; the National Museum of Photography, Bradford, UK; la Bibliothèque Nationale, Paris; the Museum of Modern Art Film Department, New York; and la Musée de la Photographie, Charleroi, Belgium.

Above left: On location in Paris. *Above right:* In her own style. *Left:* With hair stylist, Dean Cole. *Opposite:* Warmly wrapped in a blanket on set with director Richard Quine. Photos by Bob Willoughby.

Above: Photographer Bob Willoughby
with director Richard Quine.
Below: With Tony Curtis.
Opposite above: With William Holden,
Hubert de Givenchy and Mel Ferrer.
Opposite below: With William Holden
and Italian actress Capucine.
Photos by Bob Willoughby.

Above left: With Tony Curtis and Robert Wagner. *Above right:* With Noel Coward and William Holden. *Opposite left:* Jack Lemmon and William Holden.
Opposite right: With William Holden.
Photos by Bob Willoughby.

COVERING HEPBURN

Throughout her career Audrey Hepburn's image graced many magazine covers worldwide and she was photographed for countless fashion features. The following examples represent pictures by renowned photographers that helped create Hepburn's signature look during the Paramount years.

NORMAN PARKINSON (1913–1990) started out as an apprentice in a surprisingly uncreative environment, working for courtroom photographers Speaight and Sons Ltd. At the age of twenty-one he opened his own studio with Norman Kibblewhite and began to work on *The Bystander* and the British edition of *Harper's Bazaar*. During his long career, which spanned seven decades, Parkinson contributed to various other international magazines such as *Queen*, *Town and Country* and also *Vogue*, for which he was the portrait and fashion photographer from 1945 until 1960. Almost two metres tall, with an eccentric moustache and personality to match, Norman Parkinson had a remarkable ability to bring humour and elegance to his art. He challenged the more traditional fashion shoot, taking the model out of the studios.

Left: Photograph of Hepburn leaving Paramount Studios in 1953, by Bob Willoughby. *Opposite:* Hepburn was photographed by Norman Parkinson for a feature article in *Glamour* magazine in 1955.

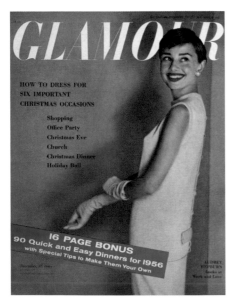

Cosmopolitan, February 1957
Photo by Richard Avedon.

Jours De France, January 27th 1962

Vogue, November 1st 1964
Photo by Irving Penn.

Glamour, December 1955
Photo by Norman Parkinson.

Life, April 19th 1954
Photo by Mark Shaw.

Harper's Bazaar, April 1956
Photo by Richard Avedon.

Harper's

BAZAAR

April 1956

Incorporating Junior Bazaar

FLOWERS:
IN FASHION
IN ART
IN BEAUTY

60 cents

Hepburn looks at a cover story about herself in the Japanese movie magazine *Screen*. Since Japanese magazines begin at what Westerners would call the end, the cover picture of Hepburn appears to be on the 'back' of the magazine.
Opposite: Screen, August 1961.
Photo by John Springer.

JAPAN'S GREATEST MOVIE MAGAZINE "SCREEN" AUGUST 1961

スクリーン

SCREEN

特集・スタアと水着
夏の話題作への招待
西部劇ヒーロー探訪
さよなら、クーパア

8

AUDREY HEPBURN

Born in Latvia, **PHILIPPE HALSMAN** (1906–1979) moved to Paris in the 30s where he began working as a photographer for *Vogue* and various other fashion magazines. But with the invasion of Hitler's army in 1940, Halsman was desperate to leave France and join his family, who had already emigrated to America. With the help of family friend Albert Einstein, he obtained a visa and moved to New York. He arrived in the Big Apple in 1940, with just a camera, very little English and no contacts. Yet within two years he was photographing for *Vogue* and *Life* magazines.

During his career he photographed 101 covers for *Life,* setting a record that still stands. From 1941 Halsman began a thirty-year collaboration with Salvador Dali. Their mutual fascination with the concept of suspension in mid-air brought them together to work on the book *Dali's Mustache.* Halsman's most famous photograph, 'Dali Atomicus', epitomises this idea of suspension by capturing an image that combined three cats, Salvador Dali jumping in mid-air and also a bucket of thrown water. From the 40s his portraits of important personalities were used in some of the leading European and American magazines. In his time he photographed Alfred Hitchcock, Winston Churchill, Marilyn Monroe and Pablo Picasso, among others. His portrait of Albert Einstein was later used in 1966 on an 8-cent US postage stamp. A lover of humour, in the 50s he took stills of Bob Hope and Groucho Marx in action telling jokes. This inspired him to take his famous 'celebrity jumping' images, such as those of the Duke and Duchess of Windsor and of Richard Nixon. By taking important figures – often from the prosperous American high society – and making them jump, he would capture them in a state that could not be posed. Halsman held many exhibitions internationally and won numerous photography awards.

Left: Life magazine, July 18th, 1955.
Photo by Philippe Halsman.
Opposite: Hepburn 'jumping' photograph by Philippe Halsman, 1955.

Photos by Philippe Halsman, 1955.

ACKNOWLEDGMENTS AND CREDITS

Andy Johnson has photographed the posters in all the books I have worked on and the quality of his work remains faultless. He has always been there when we have needed him and his contribution is immeasurable. Joakim Olsson and all the crew at the DPC have worked tirelessly on the layouts for this book and I am thankful for their dedication to this project. Leslie Gardner has been my agent since my first book over ten years ago and I am forever grateful that I have her in my life. This book would never have come to fruition if it weren't for her. I am equally indebted to Bruce Marchant, my partner at The Reel Poster Gallery, simply for being there and giving me the freedom to work on projects such as this. His presence is invaluable. My thanks also go to Alison Aitchison, our gallery co-ordinator. Early this year Kim Goddard, my assistant for seven years, decided to move abroad. Kim had worked on this project since 2003 researching, writing and organising information as it came in and co-ordinating the logistics. Her input and light-heartedness are greatly missed. My partner, Roxanna (Rocky) Hajiani, picked up this project where Kim left off and has seen it through its disorganised road to completion. Through the years and even before we had a gallery, Rocky's continual help and advice on any project or decision I have been facing have been beyond measure. Without her, I know I would not be who I am today.

Thanks to the following friends and colleagues for their continual help and support: Tarek and Basma AbuZayyad, Richard and Barbara Allen, Joe Burtis, Farhad Amirahmadi, Amit and Vanisha Bhatia, Paula Block (Paramount), Glyn Callingham, Yoshikazu Inoue, Eric and Prim Jean-Baptiste, John and Billie Kisch, Jose Ma. Carpio, Manuel Muñoz López, Mahtab Moayeri, Howard Nourmand, Gabriella Pantucci, Walt Reed, Jens Reinheimer, Daniel Strebin, The Crew from the Island, Mark and Helen Watterson, Serge and Florence Zreik; also Gordon Wise and Natalie Jerome who first approached me with this project, my former editor Jacqui Butler, Jon Butler who replaced her and saw this project through to the end and Richard Milner at Boxtree.

I also want to thank the individuals at the following agencies and institutions for their invaluable help: Dave Kent, Angela Levin (The Kobal Collection), Cristina Munoz (MPTV), Ron Harvey, Kate Anthony (Everett Collection), Faye Thompson, Anne Coco, Matt Severson, Kristine Krueger, Jenny Romero, Janet Lorenz (Academy of Motion Picture Arts and Sciences), Jacquelene Foster, Eric Rachlis (Getty Images), Miguel Lamas (Magnum Photos), Mark Lynch (Christie's Images) and Maria Johnson (The Reel Poster Archive).

Photographic credits: 3: Getty Images/Paramount, 4: Paramount/The Kobal Collection, 7: bfi stills, 9: Courtesy of the Academy of Motion Picture Arts and Sciences, 11: Getty Images, 13 & 16 Paramount/The Kobal Collection, 18: bfi stills, 19: Paramount/The Kobal Collection, 22: bfi stills, 24: Courtesy of The Everett Collection, 28: Top left and centre Courtesy of the Academy of Motion Picture Arts and Sciences; top right Courtesy of The Reel Poster Gallery, 29: © 1978 Bob Willoughby/MPTV.net, 32: © Bob Willoughby/MPTV.net, 33: © 1978 Bob Willoughby/MPTV.net, 34: left © 1978 Bob Willoughby/MPTV.net right bfi stills, 35: Bettman/Corbis, 36: Courtesy of the Academy of Motion Picture Arts and Sciences, 37: Time Life Pictures/Getty Images, 40: 1954 MPTV.net, 42: top © 2000 Mark Shaw/MPTV.net, bottom left bfi stills, 43: Courtesy of the Academy of Motion Picture Arts and Sciences, 44: Underwood & Underwood/Corbis, 45: Christie's Images, 47: Courtesy of The Everett Collection, 49: Christie's Images, 50: All photos © 1978 Bob Willoughby/MPTV.net, 51: Paramount/The Kobal Collection, 52: All © 2000 Mark Shaw/MPTV.net, 53: © Mark Shaw/MPTV.net, 54–55: Dennis Stock/Magnum Photos, 57: Courtesy of the Academy of Motion Picture Arts and Sciences, 59: 1961 MPTV.net, 64: Courtsey of The Everett Collection, 66: Paramount/The Kobal Collection, 71: Courtsey of NewsCom, 72–73: All David Seymour/Magnum Photos, 74: Getty Images, 75: bfi stills, 76: All Paramount/The Kobal Collection, 78: Paramount/The Kobal Collection, 80: Courtesy of the Academy of Motion Picture Arts and Sciences, 81: Paramount/The Kobal Collection, 82: Paramount/The Kobal Collection, 84: 1956 Paramount, 85: 1956 Paramount, 86: 1956 MPTV.net/Paramount, 87: 1956 MPTV.net/Paramount, 88: Paramount/The Kobal Collection, 91: Getty Images, 92: 1956 Paramount, 93: 1956 MPTV.net/ Paramount, 97: Paramount/The Kobal Collection, 100: bfi stills, 102: 1961 MPTV.net/Paramount, 103: Paramount/The Kobal Collection, 106: top, Gene Lester/Getty Images, bottom Rex Features, 108: Corbis, 110–111: Paramount/The Kobal Collection, 112–113: The Everett Collection, 116–117: Paramount/The Kobal Collection, 120: Courtesy of the Academy of Motion Picture Arts and Sciences, 122: Paramount/The Kobal Collection, 124: Paramount/The Kobal Collection, 125: Courtesy of the Academy of Motion Picture Arts and Sciences, 126: both Paramount/The Kobal Collection, 127: Courtesy of VinMag Archive/Elle Magazine, 129: © 1978 Bob Willoughby/MPTV.net, 130: left © 1978 Bob Willoughby/MPTV.net, right David Lees/Time Life Pictures/Getty Images, 131: David Seymour/Magnum Photos, 132: left, Bettman/Corbis; right, Chris Moore, 133: left, Corbis, right, Chris Moore, 134: left, John Springer Collection/Corbis, right, Chris Moore, 135: left, Chris Moore; right, Bettman/Corbis, 138: Paramount/The Kobal Collection, 140: © 1978 Bob Willoughby/MPTV.net, 142: bfi stills, 146: Keystone/Gamma, 147–148: © 1978 Bob Willoughby/MPTV.net, 149: bfi stills, 150–156: All © 1978 Bob Willoughby/MPTV.net, 157: Corbis, 160: Bettman/Corbis, 162: Time Life Pictures/Getty Images and Philippe Halsman/Magnum Photos, 163–167: Philippe Halsman/Magnum Photos, 168: Pele Coll/Gamma, 30, 31, 41, 48, 49, 56, 67, 79, 83, 107, 119, 121, 123, 139, 158, 159, 161: All courtesy of The Reel Poster Archive.

Photo by Philippe Halsman, 1955.